Our Future Uncovered Agenda 2030-2050

Globalist NWO & WEF secrets leaked!

The Great Reset – Economic Crisis – Global Shortages

Rebel Press Media

Disclaimer

Vax slaughter EU, including among young people: 38,000 killed and 1.6 million with serious health damage

Despite the established fact that the official European database EudraVigilance historically reflects only 6% of the actual number of vax victims, the official figures after roughly 1 year of 'vaccinating' against 'Covid-19' are nothing short of chilling: 37,927 deaths and 3,392,632 people with health damage, of which about half (over 1.6 million) are serious / permanent (such as heart disease, thrombosis, autoimmune disorders, deafness, blindness, birth defects, death). Younger people and even children in particular fall in large numbers. The mostly serious side effects and consequences - for example, in the Netherlands, Belgium and (ex-EU state) Great Britain alone there are 50,000 reports of women and girls with menstrual disorders - are invariably downplayed. Politics and media are still perpetuating the (self-)murder cult they initiated by continuing to promote and enforce these life-threatening injections on a daily basis.

The figures on January 15 from the four largest manufacturers, showing that the AstraZeneca vaccine gives the highest risk of serious side effects, and the Moderna vaccine is the most lethal. Numerically, the Pfizer vaccine makes the most victims.

Various in-depth studies of the statistics revealed last year that the EU accounted for approximately 21% of the number of reports, which would amount to 7964 dead countrymen and 712,453 people with adverse reactions, of which 338,399 with serious health damage. The number of Covid vax deaths would thus be equivalent to a hefty flu year, and the number of people with serious health harms would together now make up the fifth largest city in the country.

Get yourself a calculator to see what the figures would be if the 6% of the actual numbers mentioned earlier are taken into account. Perhaps the supposedly 'mysterious' excess mortality in the EU in recent months, the highest since WW2, comes from an angle that politics and the media are still not allowed to name? Never mind the fact that everywhere the victims are getting younger and younger:

* In Portugal, where 90.2% of the population has been injected, a 6 year old boy has died, just days after his first Pfizer shot. Authorities acknowledge the suspected serious backlash;

Table of Contents

Crisis in Europe?

After talks between the U.S. and Russia in Geneva broke down yesterday, the Ukraine crisis is escalating. 200 freight trains, each carrying 50 wagons of military equipment, are on their way from Russia to Belarus, or have already arrived there. The White House is going to step up military aid to regime in Kiev, such as providing Mi-17 helicopters, and is looking at options to strengthen the U.S. force in Eastern Europe. The Czech Republic is to supply artillery shells to Ukraine. Russia, meanwhile, warns of "the most serious consequences" if the U.S./NATO continues to refuse to meet the Kremlin's security demands - such as fulfilling promises made, notably not including Ukraine in NATO.

American radio host Hall Turner believes that there may be only one week left to avoid war with Russia. This is because that is when the Russians' ultimatum to NATO to respond in writing to the security assurances Moscow wants will expire. Meanwhile, NATO is sending large quantities of weapons to Ukraine. Earlier, the Americans stationed some 1,000 tanks and many dozens of F-15s and F'16s in Romania and other Eastern European countries.

'Anyone with half a functioning brain can see where this is going: BOEM. And we will have ourselves to blame for that because we have not kept our own governments under control,' Turner writes. 'If the people of America and Western Europe don't shower their elected representatives with phone calls, letters and emails to stop this nonsense, we could fall plumb off the cliff into the abyss.'

Yesterday afternoon (local time), the U.S. Air Force Command sent 20 ultra-priority messages in a matter of hours. These amount to "stop what you are doing now, and go do this or that. This communication system is used to activate nuclear forces and put them in a high state of readiness.

This is how WW3 could occur

Based on, among other things, his contacts with intelligence analysts, Turner describes a scenario how World War III could break out. According to him, it could start with a Russian military operation in Ukraine (possibly intended to protect the Russian population from the regular shelling by the Ukrainian army, and/or from a 'liberation' operation of De Krim, whether or not directed by the US/NATO). Then Poland comes to the rescue and attacks the Russian enclave of Kaliningrad to force the Russians to fight on two fronts.

Lithuania, Latvia, and Estonia are forced to come to Poland's aid by attacking Russian auxiliary forces threatening to cross into Kaliningrad from Belarus. Hungary and Romania are joining the fray, as are Finland and Sweden. Russia must fully mobilize to fight back on so many fronts, and conducts a total invasion of Ukraine.

This threatens to crush British troops in Ukraine. To save them, Boris Johnson orders a tactical nuclear attack on the Russian army in Ukraine. Russia retaliates with a nuclear bomb on the Ukrainian army as well as on London. Russia has been falsely blamed for everything for years, so it certainly is now. After the destruction of London the Western media scream for a tough intervention by NATO. That will come, and World War III is a fact.

West guilty of current crisis

It all started with the CIA/MI6-directed, and EU-backed "Maidan" coup in 2014 against the democratically elected president of Ukraine. Then the West installed a puppet regime in Kiev affiliated with neo-Nazi groups. With the MH17 tragedy - either a mistake by the Ukrainian military or a deliberate false flag operation to blame Russia - the anti-Putin fire was further stoked in an extremely misleading and mendacious manner.

Causing war with Russia - the big stumbling block of the already years planned and prepared communist Great Reset / Build Back Better coup that the Western WEF regimes (like Rutte's) are now carrying out against their own peoples - was the main goal from the beginning in the medium term.

The West broke all promises and guarantees to Russia after the fall of the Wall and the collapse of the Iron Curtain. Those guarantees allowed for no war between East and West in the late 1980s, and included not expanding NATO eastward without Russian consent. However, that is what happened anyway. In fact, in the 1990s, the US/NATO led by Bill Clinton waged an illegal and bloody war against Serbia (then part of Yugoslavia) only because it had remained an ally of Russia. Then other allies of Moscow, such as Libya and Syria, were also targeted.

Armstrong: 'Putin can conquer Europe in the blink of an eye'

The American top economist Martin Armstrong writes that Putin is capable of 'conquering Europe in the blink of an eye'. Seldom have we been so weak, and that by our own hand, because we have endangered our stable energy supply by the useless but extremely expensive switch to unreliable 'sustainable' sources. Germany will only have natural gas in reserve for a little over two weeks when Russia, in retaliation for the possible heavier economic sanctions now threatened by the EU, turns off the gas tap.

In a shielded commentary, Armstrong writes that IF Russia and China ever want to defeat the West militarily, they should seize their opportunity NOW. If they take advantage of this unique opportunity, that attack (by Russia on Europe and China on Taiwan/Japan/Australia, and jointly on the U.S.) should occur between late February and late March.

No major conventional war, but sudden massive nuclear attack?

My own hypothetical scenario looks different from that of Turner or Armstrong. I personally think that the strategically brilliant Putin will not be lured into a major conventional war with the West. The massive Russian mobilizations are, in my view, just a diversionary tactic. Perhaps his troops will still engage in combat in Ukraine, but the real thump, in my view, will come from the nuclear submarines, quietly moved into position, which will strike simultaneously and totally destroy the United States and Europe (and in the East Japan, Taiwan, South Korea and Australia) in one fell swoop with Chinese help.

And again: IF this happens, the blame for this will lie entirely with the unfathomably arrogant and now purely lying war-haters in Washington, Brussels and London. Russia tried to join NATO three times, but the US in particular would not. The Pentagon needed enemies to continue justifying its monstrous military spending.

Prophecy: 'They will cry out for peace, but get destruction'

Now the leaders of both America and Europe 'need' a war for yet another reason, namely to cover up the fact that in propping up the banks at the expense of their own constituents' prosperity and with their devastating but utterly pointless climate and lockdown measures they have bankrupted their own societies and economies and brought them to the brink of destruction.

'While they are crying out (in the vein of "demanding" or "commanding"): peace and rest! a sudden destruction comes upon them, like the contractions of a pregnant woman, and they will by no means escape.' (1 Tess.5:3. the correct statement from the original text. No condition of 'peace and rest' is described here, but a 'call' OM peace, during a period of great tension and worldwide fear. (See also Luke 21:25-26 about the end times: "...on the earth a desperate fear is spreading among the peoples...and people are trembling with fear and dread over the things that are coming to the world.)

Has the time of fulfillment now indeed come near, and is man given over to his relentless urge for total domination and/or total destruction of 'the other'? Or will this insane world get one more (last?) merciful, but in my opinion undeserved, reprieve.

Chinese colonel warns US: If you come to Taiwan's aid, an all-out nuclear war will follow

Is the war against US/EU/NATO planned by Putin for years about to break out? We have written many times that such a life-threatening military conflict could very well start with a "false flag" operation, intended to place the blame on the EU. And what about the following serious American provocation: a National Airlines cargo plane under military command, which had just delivered a whole load of ammunition to Kiev, suddenly chose a completely different course after takeoff, violated the airspace of Belarus, and then flew hundreds of kilometers through Russian airspace, roughly right over the Russian army units that have been assembled for a possible war with Ukraine. Near Kazakhstan, the aircraft disappeared from flight tracking radar.

Were the Russians hoping they would bring down the cargo plane, giving them their desired pretext for taking the next step toward starting a war? At least the Kremlin does not seem to have fallen into this trap.

Su-57 stealth fighter over Kiev?

Then followed something even more remarkable. On the same flight tracking, a Russian Su-57 stealth fighter appeared out of nowhere over Kiev. At a height of only

350 meters, the aircraft flew several kilometers over the city, and then 'disappeared' without a trace. '

If this incident actually happened, it must have made a huge noise in the Ukrainian capital. It would have been an unprecedented display of power on the part of the Russians, and a message that could put the West in particular in its pocket, since Russian stealth technology is evidently much more advanced than previously thought, and capable of completely evading Western radar systems.

According to the Pentagon, Russia has moved two divisions of S-400 missile defense systems and an unknown number of fighter jets to Belarus, which means that "Kiev is now in the crosshairs. Meanwhile, family members of "non-essential staff & diplomats" are being evacuated from Ukraine, which the Biden administration says is only a "preventive measure.

Chinese colonel threatens US with all-out nuclear war

Tensions with China are also being further escalated by the Americans. Last Thursday, the Chinese Navy expelled the USS Benfold from the territorial waters of the disputed Xisha Islands (Western name: Paracel Islands) in the South China Sea.

Regardless of who these islands might belong to, the continuous "patrolling" of U.S. warships so close to China is an outright provocation. How would

Washington react if there were continuous Chinese warships passing through the Gulf of Mexico?

In Beijing, therefore, people are getting angrier. A high-ranking colonel of the PLA (the army) warned on state broadcaster CCTV that the US should not dare to come to Taiwan's aid during a military conflict. This, he said, would immediately lead to the destruction of the U.S. aircraft carriers in the region, and an all-out nuclear war.

'After cyber attack, we will lose our access to the internet' - 'Live Free or Die' now more applicable than ever

The WEF (false flag) cyber attack resulting in a massive blackout in Europe, intended to push through the Great Reset while framing Russia and having a pretext for unleashing World War III, seems close at hand as major countries in Central Asia were hit yesterday by a massive power outage affecting millions. Lights, water, toilets, refrigerators, heating - nothing worked anymore. Countless people got stuck in elevators and ski elevators. Traffic degenerated into chaos. Considering the Western-induced war tensions around Ukraine, the period February-March could become very exciting in this respect as well, especially if it is considered that exactly in this period the EU will 'practice' for 6 weeks on a so-called 'Russian cyber-attack'.

Kazakhstan - recently the target of a failed 'Maidan' like MI6 coup attempt -, Uzbekistan and Kyrgyzstan, three former Soviet republics whose electricity grids are connected to Russia, were left without power yesterday, according to the Kazakhstan Electricity Operating Company (KEGOC) due to a sudden imbalance in the grid. In Tashkent, the capital of Uzbekistan, subways came to a halt and the airport had to be shut down. Residents of the country reported failing water supplies and heating. Bishkek, the capital of Kyrgyzstan, came to a complete standstill. Traffic became chaos, many people complained of heating failures.

Some speculate that the cryptomining boom is the cause. After China began to regulate the highly energy intensive mining of cryptos, it shifted to Kazakhstan.

'After cyber attack we lose our access to the internet'

Others believe that the cyber attack from earlier this year has now affected these countries as well. In the EU, the PVD seems to be the only party that dares to say openly what is really going on.

'What is likely to happen is that there will be a "cyber-attack" or a "cyber-pandemic" - for which Russia will then be blamed. As if it were part of the strategy towards Ukraine. Because of that "cyber-attack" or "cyber-pandemic" we are going to lose our access to the Internet.

We will only get it back with an "internet passport". So I think they are going to do exactly the same trick in the digital world as they have been doing for the past 2 years in the physical world: first of all deny access under a false pretext.

(Physical world: corona, digital world: cyberattacks) and then return it 'safely and securely' with a passport. Fully integrated digital ID is then a reality. And the Great Reset has been realized one step further.'

And so the lion's share of the still sleepwalking population, including the US, is being led by the WEF and its subordinate Western regimes, into the next planned mega-crisis designed to push through the communist Great Reset / Build Back Better / Agenda-2030, which threatens to become the harshest and most inhumane dictatorship that has ever plagued our planet.

Live Free or Die

At least, if World War III doesn't end it prematurely. At this stage, that would even be a lesser outcome. After all: It's better to die free than live life in a cage , even if that cage is a digital one. (* A paraphrase of Emiliano Zapata's 'It is better to die on your feet than to live on your knees). 'Live Free or Die' has been the motto of the U.S. state of New Hampshire for 77 years, and should also be the motto of all people who still place some value on freedom, self-determination and respect for others.

"Is life so dear, or peace so sweet, as to be purchased at the price of chains and slavery? Forbid it, Almighty God! I know not what course others may take; but as for me, give me liberty or give me death!" (Patrick Henry, 1775)

The politicians and other authorities who keep on promising you that you will get your freedom back if you just meet all kinds of requirements (injections, QR codes, mouth caps, etc.), plus the people who obey

them as fearfully as they blindly, can therefore very well
be described by the following text:

Freedom they pretend to be, though they themselves
are slaves of perdition; for he by whom one is
overpowered is one's slave. (2 Peter 2:19)

First communist world dictatorship to become a reality by 2022 - Injecting every earth inhabitant top priority number 1 - Current prosperity to be largely dismantled - UN seeks permanent end to freedom of speech and science

The UN Secretary General, Portuguese communist António Guterres, is demanding that the whole world move to a permanent global state of emergency this year because of Covid-19 and the climate. And you thought that everything was on its way back to normal, now that you can go to the pub again. But we have not yet experienced anything of what the UN, WHO, WEF and IMF all have in store, and what is being announced more and more openly: an unprecedentedly harsh global dictatorship in which we will no longer have any freedom or control over our lives, not even our own bodies.

'We must tackle these threats together, based on unity and solidarity,' Guterres declared in his address to the General Assembly earlier this month. There must be a "full mobilization of all countries" to address a "five alarm situations," namely Covid-19, the climate, a morally bankrupt financial system, "lawlessness in cyberspace," and declining peace and security in the world.

Stopping Covid and injecting everyone top priority No. 1

Stopping the supposed coronavirus (scientifically impossible anyway and also completely unnecessary medically) is the absolute top priority, according to Guterres. For form's sake, he added that Covid must not be used to undermine human rights, restrict civil rights and impose disproportionate restrictions, which of course has already happened and is still going on, precisely on the orders of the UN health agency, the WHO.

The UN leader added the now infamous and infinitely repeated glass-hard lies, "Our actions must be based on science and common sense. The science is clear: vaccines work. Vaccines save lives.' Therefore, the so-called 'vaccine inequality' should be eliminated as soon as possible; by the end of 2021, 40% of the world's population had been injected (= genetically engineered), by the middle of 2022 this should rise to 70%.

In Africa, however, that percentage will not be reached until 2024. 'Instead of the virus spreading like wildfire, the vaccine should do that,' Guterres said, pointing out that 1.5 billion doses are produced every month, but that the distribution of these around the world is 'scandalously uneven.'

He forgot to mention that the countries so 'disadvantaged' with 'vaccines' are hardly, if at all, affected by Covid-19, and the countries with the highest vaccination rates invariably report the highest numbers of sick and dead. Real science has therefore long since proven that vaccines = Covid-19. (See Covid section for the numerous articles and links on this).

Everyone soon to be equally poor under UN/WHO/WEF world government

The second alarm applies to the "reform of the global financial system. Once again, socialist credos are trotted out that all sound very nice and true, such as the fact that in the current system the rich are rewarded and the poor are punished. His "solution"? One centralized global financial system, when centralization/globalization has actually led to the enormous inequality.

The 'better support of developing countries' and 'a fairer global tax system' therefore amounts to a massive forced transfer of wealth from rich to poor, a massive levelling of billions of people. End result: everyone equally poor, except of course for the members of the Big Finance, Big Tech and Big Pharme controlled UN/ WHO/ WEF/ IMF world government, who are in the process of getting their hands on ALL wealth and prosperity, and thus total control over everyone.

Prosperity largely aborted for non-existent CO2 crisis

All countries have "no choice" to go into a state of emergency to solve the "climate crisis," the racial communist continued. Global emissions of CO2 - which in reality are still at historically, almost dangerously low levels, and have nothing at all to do with the mild, stagnant global warming, which in the real world has even reversed into global cooling - must be reduced by 45% by 2030. To do this, fossil energy sources (oil, gas, coal), the basis of our current prosperity, must be largely demolished.

The massive, wealth-destroying investments required for the "green transition" must triple to $5 trillion a year by 2030. However, rich countries still have to fulfill their promise to give $100 billion to developing countries by 2022 to meet climate targets there.

'Fighting infodemics' = End of freedom of expression

The fourth alert is the "growing digital chaos" that would be exploited by the "most destructive forces. Would Guterres have looked in the mirror? Because while he rightly points to the 'exploitation of our personal info to manipulate us, change our behavior, violate our human rights and undermine democratic institutions', he then wants to reserve exactly these 'rights' exclusively for the United Nations.

'Our choices are being taken away from us without us even realizing it.' Indeed, Mr. Guterres - precisely by the UN, the WHO, the WEF, the IMF, and all the other globalist agencies. You are the ones advocating a world dictatorship based on your pandemic and climate hoax. You are the ones who supposedly want to end the 'infodemic' and the - in reality waged by you - 'war on science', thus ending freedom of speech and freedom of independent scientific research - exactly as it happens everywhere and always in communist states.

r

With the world experiencing the highest number of violent conflicts since 1945, the call for peace and security (/ 'peace and tranquility') is louder than ever. Naturally, 'populism' (= the will of peoples to remain free and independent and to determine their own course) is seen as one of the greatest dangers.

'Fighting terrorism' is also mentioned again. The by far most dangerous terrorist organizations that have endangered the entire planet - Pentagon / NATO and the WEF, not to mention WHO = the UN itself - are naturally left out. Advocating for the deployment of UN troops and money to ensure "human rights, especially for women and girls" in Afghanistan is extremely wry and also ludicrous given the recent humiliating US/NATO retreat from that country.

Finally, Guterres emphasized that unity in the UN Security Council is sorely needed to address all these 'challenges', and that women leaders must be central to 'conflict prevention and peace-making'. We saw and are seeing from types like Angela Merkel, Christine Lagarde, Jacinda Ardern, Hillary Clinton and Victoria Nuland that women in leadership positions really do not always guarantee less lies and intrigue, more transparency and more humanity and peace - quite the opposite.

23

Conclusion: the free world is no more. Communism won after all. It is only cold comfort that historically all communist countries and systems eventually collapse, because you cannot keep suppressing humans and human nature indefinitely. Unfortunately, such a collapse is always accompanied by huge numbers of victims, and this time will be no different.

Global Cooling: Thick pack of snow in Jerusalem; Seawater near Greece frozen

In absolute obedience to the actually already functioning feudalist UN world government, also the EU regime still bases its climate-energy policy on the proven hoax that anthropogenic CO_2 causes global warming; a 'warming' that in reality has not existed for years. On the contrary, the new solar minimum, in combination with the rapidly diminishing magnetic field and the coincidence of the end of all climate cycles (which always heralds a new Ice Age), has set in motion a period of global cooling, which is many times more dangerous and harmful for humanity than a predicted fictitious warming of 2 degrees Celsius at the end of this century. The countless evidences of this cooling are visible all over the world, but are distorted or ignored by politics and media.

USA: 'Worst snowstorm in history'

75 million residents of the US East Coast are bracing themselves for what meteorologists say will be "the worst blizzard in history," which, according to a CNN meteorologist, can only be compared "to the most powerful hurricane. Yesterday, 2,000 flights were already cancelled due to this "bomb cyclone," and today nearly 3,500 more. A snow layer of 45 to possibly 75 centimeters is expected.

Also in southern Florida this weekend it will not be this cold since the 60's, and early this week a warning was even issued for night frost. In the state of Kansas, 68 inches of snow fell this week; in some places, the record of 76 inches was broken. Colorado also experienced a snowstorm (4). In Nashville, Tennessee, 23.6 inches of snow fell from the sky between January 1 and January 21, the largest amount since 1985.

Elsewhere, cold and snow are the order of the day

* In the tourist southeast of Turkey (Antalya, Mugla, Dalaman) the first snow since 1993 has fallen. Last weekend parts of Istanbul received a layer of one meter. It was never so cold in the country, in some places almost -40. There were also record amounts of snow. The government was forced to make the decision to partially cut off the electricity 3 days a week because it could no longer provide sufficient energy;

Rare thick pack of snow in Jerusalem; frost in Sahara desert

It sometimes snows in and around Jerusalem, but rarely did it fall as thick as last Thursday. Roads, schools and businesses had to be closed. Many residents tweeted that they had never experienced this before in their entire lives.

Snow even fell in the Sahara desert, which has only happened 5 times before in the past 43 years (and - given global cooling - not entirely coincidentally in 2016,

2018, 2021 and now 2022). In Ain Sefra (Algeria) it froze -2 degrees.

Seawater freezes off Greece

Greek media are talking about a "once in a lifetime phenomenon": Just off the coast of the country, sea ice has been found, which you normally only find in the polar seas. Near the coastal town of Sagiada, the westernmost point of Greece where there is a Mediterranean climate, the temperature dropped to almost - 20 C.

Athens - the warmest capital in the EU - was covered in a record layer of snow during the heaviest blizzard since 1968, and the popular vacation island of Mykonos also turned white. 44 Greek weather stations measured unprecedented low temperatures ranging from -10 to - 18.

* Turkey's neighbors Iran (-27.4) and Iraq (-30) also experienced extreme cold last weekend; record domestic demand forced Iran to scale back gas deliveries to Turkey, which could not have come at a worse time for that country. UN officials spoke of "horror conditions" in refugee camps because of Syria's freezing cold and snow. Children walked barefoot through the snow wearing only sandals, and must survive in thin, torn tents;

* Even in India it is particularly chilly; in Delhi the official temperature on Tuesday did not exceed 12.1 degrees,

which is 10 degrees lower than the average. Last month there were already 11 days with temperatures below 17 C.. Meteorologists expect winter records to be broken in 2003;

As it gets colder, Europe breaks down stable and affordable energy

Continued very low temperatures are expected for the Caucasus, Ukraine, Turkey, the Middle East and Northeast Africa, which will further increase the already unprecedented demand for energy and will make the energy crisis in Europe, mainly caused by the divestment of oil/gas and nuclear power plants, and the switch to very expensive and very unreliable (especially during cold) 'renewable' energy sources such as wind and solar, even more acute, plunging millions of people into deep poverty, which many of the weakest will probably not survive.

Techno dimensional future?

Our article series 'Forbidden Gates: The beginning of the techno-dimensional war' in 2010 was still considered by many to be pure science fiction, something that lay far in the future. Please re-read some parts in this article, and see for yourself that what seemed like SF at the time is becoming hard - and I would say especially sinister - reality, especially with the Covid gene manipulation/graphene oxide injections, the QR code, AI and 5G. 'We are going to change you,' WEF top executive Klaus Schwab openly announced a few years ago. And that is exactly what has been done on a massive scale worldwide since the late 2020s. Refusers to this totalitarian bio/tech control in the making, which will put an end to all our freedoms, human rights and privacy, will soon be completely expelled from society.

(August 16, 2010 ***): Scientific laboratories around the world have long been working on revolutionary technologies that will change not only our brains, our memories and our bodies, but according to author Joel Garreau (book Radical Evolution) even our souls. The humans of the future will be unrecognizably superior to us - at least, if it's up to the scientists and intellectuals who make up the rapidly growing movement called transhumanism. Studies by some transhumanists claim that the DNA, the building blocks of human life, can be altered in such a way that we will be able to interact with as yet 'invisible intelligences'.

The crossing of the boundary between the visible and invisible worlds will test people's faith in ways never before seen. Huge numbers of believers may well be paralyzed with terror by the far-reaching supernatural consequences. The fate of many -and that of their families- may well depend on their knowledge of this new reality and whether they will have adequately prepared for it.

Plan to 'redesign' man already thousands of years old

In his new book ("Forbidden Gates"), Thomas Horn shows that there is an evil force thousands of years old behind the plans to mix humans, machines and even animals in order to redesign humanity. This power has now managed to present itself as a "progressive" and "enlightened" path to help mankind into the "next stage of evolution. As machine and 'god-like' humans are rapidly evolving, and as there is an increasing willingness to cross the God-ordained boundaries between both species and dimensions, believers will have to start preparing for a whole new way of spiritual warfare.

There is an invisible spiritual battle going on for the soul of every human being, believer and unbeliever alike. It is therefore of utmost importance to recognize the nature of this battle, as well as the tactics used by our evil enemies. It is important to realize that everyone is involved in this war, whether we like it or not. To avoid this battle is to have lost this battle in advance.

Spiritual or spiritual warfare therefore begins with the recognition that invisible "agents" and beings exist on Earth, both good and evil, and that they seek to influence both our lives at home, in church, government and society, and our personalities.

Evil has taken control of governments, agencies and societies

These evil entities (often called "demons" and "fallen angels" in religious circles) play a major role in society in influencing and controlling individuals, agencies and governments. Their close cooperation with so-called 'social architects', people and governments who are pursuing more or less the same goals -namely total domination over everything and everyone- is still denied by many who are blind to the reality of the spiritual world. Behind and through people's representatives, legislators, presidents, dictators and even religious leaders, these evil beings can freely exercise their power. As soon as a religious or political power has risen against good somewhere, they make every effort to cast it in an evil light and tear it down stone by stone, soul by soul.

In more than 30 important texts, the New Testament uses the Greek word "cosmos" to make mention of this system, this "empire," this "government behind the government. Under evil (/demonic) influence, people are given a certain power which causes their egos separated from God to become increasingly hostile to humanity, and they begin to see people as objects that can and must be manipulated and used to achieve their insane ambitions*.

(Klaus Schwab's 'Great Reset' / 'Build Back Better'; the UN's 'Agenda-2030'; Bill Gates' 'vaccination everyone', the EU's 'Green New Deal', etc..).

Some believe that this system already began with Lucifer's rebellion in heaven, when he became proud and aligned himself with God. This once exalted being then spread his unquenchable thirst for power, domination and dominance among his followers, the still active dark agents responsible for the 'cause-and-effect' principle between visible and invisible personalities.

Cosmokrators

The powers in this supernatural sphere are determined and put in place by Satan (/ Lucifer, and his many other names). He is at the head of important "cosmokrators"-rulers of darkness working in and through their human likenesses-who in turn command lower spirits so that all earthly authorities-both secular and religious-can be reached and influenced at every level.

If we could take a peek behind the scenes of this spiritual world, we would witness a battle between good and evil, with the souls of people at stake. Entire legions are vying for power over people, cities, territories, countries and even continents. The Bible testifies to this reality in Luke 4, where the devil takes

Jesus to the top of a high mountain and shows him all the kingdoms of the earth. 'And the devil said unto him, To thee do I give all this power, and their glory: for it is given unto me, and I give it unto whom I will. If then Thou dost worship me, it shall be wholly Thine.' (vs.6-7)

The apostle Paul later writes to the believers in Ephesus: '... for we have not to wrestle against blood and flesh, but against principalities, against powers, against the rulers of this darkness, against evil spirits in the heavenly places.' (Eph.66:12 *) It is there where opposition to God finds its origin. Conflicts and clashes between people, institutions and governments are therefore often the visible manifestations of a struggle that takes place in the invisible, spiritual world. ('Heavenly realms' we might call 'dimensions' in modern language).

Was 2021 the real 'year 1' of the Luciferian New World Order?

Horn discovered in his research for his book that 2012 was mentioned in various government reports as 'year 1' of the new techno-dimensional human 'improvement'. Predictive programming - with all its deceptions and hidden data - is one of the main ways Masons / Illuminati obey their 'code' to always let humanity know what their plans are. Could 2012 in reality have meant 2021 as 'year 1' of the Luciferian New World Order, the year in which with the Covid-19 gene manipulation injections began the final transformation of man into a being that will soon be forever cut off from the true Light, from God?

So realize well that it will not be another "hundreds" of years, nor will it be "decades". What occult powers have carefully prepared for thousands of years is about to reveal itself to humanity / be imposed on humanity. The clock is ticking inexorably towards the target year of 2012 (/ 2021?). Once you fully understand this you will also be able to prepare and sustain yourself ** in what will prove to be the most exhilarating and bewildering period in all of human history. (/ To be continued)

** Except for a still far too small group, the vast majority (at least 8 out of 10, regardless of faith or creed) appeared mentally and spiritually totally unprepared for this final war against humanity, which was definitively unleashed with the climate-vaccination programs (the already mentioned Agenda-2030, Great Reset, etc.). The time left to stop this diabolical agenda and try to undo the damage is very, very short.

All countries with highest Covid vax rate had very high excess mortality in 2021 - Official government data US: 15600% more heart disease among young people under 30 - CDC confirms excess mortality of 40% among 18-49 year olds by 2021

A new analysis of official U.S. VAERS data by Dr. Jessica Rose shows that the number of spontaneous abortions due to Covid-19 injections has risen to 416,186. The same government statistics show a 15600% increase in heart disease among "vaccinated" youth up to age 30.

Dr. Rose arrived at a URF of 118 (under reporting factor) in the VAERS for spontaneous abortions based on recently released (DEMD) data from the Department of Defense. As the 2021 figure stands at 3527, the actual number is 416,186. Only 1% of those were not caused by the "vaccine. (1)

Both inside and outside the VAERS, there is now more than enough evidence that the Covid injections confuse and/or damage the female reproductive organs, either temporarily or permanently. On January 21, we wrote that nearly 50,000 "vaccinated" women and girls have developed menstrual disorders in the Netherlands, Belgium and Great Britain alone.

Pregnant women were excluded from the testing phases in 2020. That the injections were recommended to pregnant women or women with an immediate desire to have children thereafter therefore amounts, at a minimum, to evil medical practices, but in fact even to crimes against humanity.

Covid injection causes 3250% more vax victims

The VAERS recorded over 1 million individual Covid vax victims on January 21, including 22,607 deaths. That number of 1 million in just over 1 year surpasses the 915,813 (including 29,542 deaths) from all other vaccines in the past 31 years combined, and represents a 3250% annual increase. Governments, media, and scientists who still claim that the Covid shot is "safe" are therefore lying through their teeth.

Of the more than 1 million who have developed health problems after their injections, 2132 young people under 30 have myocarditis or pericarditis. That number nearly doubles to 3912 if all types of heart disease are included, not just the two best known.

For all other vaccines (80+), 23 people under 30 get heart disease after their injection every year. For the Covid vaccines, the figure is 3611 people under 30 per year, a whopping 15600% increase. (2) Note that this is only the official VAERS data, which was determined years ago to include at most only 1% of the actual number of vax deaths.

CDC: Workforce Mortality 40%

We reported earlier that according to statistics from the major insurer OneAmerica, in 2021 the excess mortality rate among the U.S. working population aged 18 to 49 was 40% (see our January 3 article: Covid vaxxicide: U.S. insurers report 40% more deaths in working population) . That percentage is now confirmed by the CDC.

In most states, much of the excess mortality was automatically attributed to Covid. This is done in the same extremely misleading way as in the Netherlands; for example, if someone has had a heart attack or traffic accident, and is found to be "positive" with a false PCR test, such a person enters the statistics as a Covid victim.

The excess deaths were highest in Nevada (65% / 36% due to Covid), Texas (61%, of which 58% were Covid) and Arizona (57%, of which 37% were Covid). The District of Columbia reported an even higher mortality rate of 72%, 0% of which was by Covid.

There were nearly 6,000 additional deaths in that age group from non-Covid related pneumonia. Influenza also appeared to have taken a sudden vacation in the US (only 50 deaths), unless Covid was indeed just a new name for the flu. Many additional deaths are attributed to drugs (especially fentanyl); the number of deaths rose to 101,000 in the 12 months before June 2021. In 2019, there were "only" 72,000.

In the 50 to 84 age group, the excess mortality rate was over 27% (over 470,000 additional deaths). In almost 4 out of 5 cases, Covid was listed as the (co) cause of death.

All countries with highest Covid vax rate have very high excess mortality

'I think it is very likely that in the next phase the number of deaths will dwarf the claims of the number of Covid victims,' stated former Pfizer VP Dr. Mike Yeadon. 'Although the evidence is always circumstantial, based on the figures and statistics, he said there can be no doubt that the huge excess mortality in countries with the highest Covid vax rate is indeed caused by the injections.

The trend 'More Covid injections = More deaths' is too striking everywhere to be called 'coincidence'. In Scotland, for example, 87% of adults have been 'vaccinated'; weekly deaths are now 30% above normal. In Germany, there was 10% excess mortality at a vax rate of 80% (September 2021).

The 'mysteriously' named sharp rise in deaths in Denmark, Finland and Norway - higher than during the worst corona 'pandemic' weeks - also went hand in hand with the ever-increasing number of injections. The Netherlands, Europe's top injection country according to some statistics, even experienced the highest excess mortality rate since World War II.

Victims younger and younger

According to VigiAccess, the WHO's vax database, a staggering 41% of the 2.4 million recorded injection illnesses and deaths are under the age of 44. Only 6% are 75-plus. The Covid injections are thus causing a real slaughter among increasingly younger people, but the media are not allowed to report this. So the media only mention unproven, invented causes such as "stress from the pandemic" or the in reality very mild "Omicron variant".

Why was mortality higher in 2021 than in 'pandemic year' 2020, when there were no 'vaccinations' at all? To ask the question is to answer it: because vaccinations were in place from 2021. Global statistics undeniably show this. In Africa, there is barely any Covid, while the vax rate there is very low. Europe and the US are flooded with people with Covid symptoms, while the vax rate there is very high.

Overall mortality among vaccinated people just (much) HIGHER

'If Covid is as dangerous as claimed, and the vaccine as effective as claimed, then we should now be seeing far more Covid-related deaths among the unvaccinated than among the vaccinated,' Professor Norman Fenton (Queen Mary London University) said recently, pointing to the official ONS statistics. 'And if the vaccine is safe, as is claimed, then there should be far fewer additional deaths from causes other than Covid among vaccinated people than among unvaccinated people.'

What the professor discovered, however, was the opposite. In fact, overall mortality among vaccinated people is (much) HIGHER than among unvaccinated people. Numerous hospitals report that the masses of (vaccinated) people coming in now are much sicker than they have ever been. Even NPR acknowledged that most of these people, who come in with severe thrombosis, heart disease, organ pains and respiratory problems, among other things, do not have Covid.

Fenton hoped that a debate on this would ensue, but instead he is now suddenly dismissed as an extremist, which happens everywhere to anyone who dares to question these untouchable and 'sacred' declared gene manipulation injections openly for even a second.

'Media complicit in this mass extermination?'

In the near future (between now and 1 to 3 years), young vaccinated people may well be in for a huge wave of serious diseases. For example, the New York Post reported that experts are warning that a little-known spontaneous serious disease (SCAD) that causes a heart attack, and normally affects mostly women between 30 and 60, is now also toppling young fit women of 22.

Similar articles are appearing in an increasing number of Western media outlets that seem to be preparing the public to accept a much higher rate of illness and death by default, especially among young people. "Does it seem that the media have accepted their role as accomplices in this mass extermination, or is that an exaggeration?" the British The Exposé rightly asks.

Heart attacks everywhere?

Lawyer US reveals shocking increase in vax casualties based on claimed figures - Canadian figures confirm pandemic of vaccinated people: Effectiveness of Covid injections found to be not the claimed 95%, but MIN 425%

A new analysis of current figures and developments shows that 62.3 million people worldwide could die from heart disease by 2022 as a result of Covid-19 injections. Terms such as vaxxicide (vaccine genocide), depopulation and mass extinction are thus beginning to become more and more real. As we predicted back in 2020, these casualties will be falsely attributed to a Covid variant (or Covid-induced disease) so that people continue to line up neatly for their next booster shot.

The number of professional athletes affected by serious and/or fatal heart disease doubled every three months last year. FIFA counted 31 dead professional footballers in 2021, rising from 2 in the first quarter to 21 in the final quarter. They can be considered the proverbial canary in the coal mine. Top footballers are the first to die because they put the most strain on their hearts with constant training and the many matches. One of the most famous footballers who just survived is Sergio Aguero, who, however, will never be on the field again due to his vax heart condition.

In November 2021, we wrote about a report from the American Heart Association (AHA), which warned that within five years, vaccinated people will have a more than double chance of having a heart attack. Assuming that the explosion in heart disease set in motion last year continues at the same rate, and that the number of vaxxers (now 51.6% worldwide) does not continue to rise.

Normally, an average of 8.9 million people die each year from heart disease. At the current rate, that threatens to become 71.2 million this year, an increase of 62.3 million deaths. That means Covid injections will kill more people than HIV/AIDS, and that from heart attacks alone. This does not even count the many other identified causes of death from these mRNA gene manipulation injections, such as VAIDS (= vaccine-AIDS resulting from a demonstrated stepwise destroyed immune system) and neurological degeneration. (1)

Vaxxers can only hope that their damaged immune systems will spontaneously recover and overcome the toxic spike proteins produced by the injections into their own bodies. So far, however, there is no indication of this - quite the contrary. For months now, the trend everywhere has undeniably been in only one direction: More Injections = More Sick and Dead.

Shocking increase in serious illnesses and diseases among core healthy military personnel

This is confirmed by, among others, the (DMED) figures from the US Department of Defense. Attorney Thomas Renz has been working for months on behalf of the vax victims ignored and left to their own devices by politicians, media and the medical community. Last Monday, at a hearing with Senator Ron Johnson, he presented the shocking statistics, leaked by military doctors who could no longer stand the staggering number of young healthy military personnel who have developed serious illnesses and other medical complaints after their "vaccinations.

According to them, the Covid injections in the military have now caused the following:

* 300% more miscarriages in female soldiers (4182, compared to the normal five-year average of 1499);

* nearly 300% more cancer diagnoses (114645 in the first 11 months of 2021, compared to normal 38700 per year)

* 1000% more neurological disorders (from normal 82,000 to 863,000 last year);

* 269% more myocardial infarctions;

* 291% more frequent Bell's palsy (facial paralysis);

* 156% more birth defects (of children of military personnel);

* 471% more frequent infertility in female military personnel;

* 467% more pulmonary embolisms.

In an affidavit, one of the military whistleblowers states that "it is my professional opinion that the most significant increases in the above discussed cases of miscarriages, cancers and diseases were caused by Covid-19 vaccinations. (Noting that one vaccinated person may have been affected by more than one of the conditions mentioned, and therefore the percentages are based on the number of diagnoses, not the number of individual cases).

Renz says the burden of proof is on the government, not the other way around, especially since both military personnel and civilians are forced to be injected with an experimental product whose manufacturers are exempt from any liability in advance. If the injections are at all "safe and effective," as is still being claimed, then the Pentagon should have no problem explaining the cause of this gigantic increase in diseases, disorders, and illnesses. (2)

Canada: Vaccines have NEGATIVE effectiveness of 425%

And that this real cause seems to be the injections themselves is also shown by careful independent analysis of the official data of the Canadian government. Instead of a claimed effectiveness of 95%, the "vaccines" have a NEGATIVE effectiveness of 425% in fully vaccinated people as young as 12 years old. As many as 89% of all new cases attributed to Covid in January were fully vaccinated.

Pfizer arrived at 95% via a now infamous misleading calculation method, namely by plotting during the test phase the number of corona infections in the placebo group (162) against the number of infections in the 'vaccinated' group (8). A much fairer picture would have been painted if these numbers of so-called 'infections' had been set against the total tested group of 21830 people. Indeed, the difference would then be only 0.7%.

Many national governments used a similar dirty trick in their monthly "infection" statistics by reporting the total number of unvaccinated people from the very beginning of the vax campaign (December 2020/January 2021). By doing so, they gave the false impression that the lion's share of 'infections' were unvaccinated.

However, thanks to the internet archive, it is possible to find out exactly what the real figures are. In the above case of Canada, between December 21 and January 22, there were 49579 'cases' among unvaccinated people, and a huge number of 390401 among vaccinated people. From this follows a staggering 'vaccine' effectiveness rate of -425%.

Injections based on a computer model 'virus'

Again, these data prove that the Covid-19 injections actually make people much more susceptible to disease symptoms attributed to Covid. We purposely keep describing it this way, since the CSO of Novavax acknowledged in front of the cameras late last year that they do NOT have access to a 'live' virus, but only a computer model. In other words, the gene manipulation 'vaccines' have been formulated based on Chinese-supplied (genetic) lab information of a supposed coronavirus claimed to cause Covid-19.

We have been writing since early 2021 that it looks suspiciously like Covid-19 is actually caused by the injections (something we predicted back in 2020, by the way). But "all those sick then in 2020"? First, there appeared to have been no excess mortality in that year. Second, the number of IC/ hospital admissions in the EU was lower than in the previous five years. Thirdly, the normal flu in that year suddenly and unnaturally almost disappeared, and the supposed 'corona patients' all had symptoms that would have been attributed to influenza in any other year. For example, the standard PCR tests also used in the EU were banned in the US as of January 1 because they cannot distinguish between corona and influenza.

The question asked by more and more people whether we have not been gigantically conned since 2020 with a fake 'pandemic', which was only invented as a pretext to subject the entire world to a totalitarian communist UN/WHO/WEF/IMF climate-vaccination dictatorship, can therefore without a trace of doubt be answered with YES.

Super HIV in the EU?

Official Canadian government figures (immune systems downgraded to average MIN 81% thanks to injections) indicate upcoming AIDS outbreak among fully vaccinated.

Do you remember our earlier books on the link between the immune system undermining Covid injections and the emergence of a new form of AIDS? Well, American media reported a few days ago that scientists have discovered a virulent 'VB variant' of HIV ('super HIV') in the Netherlands (1). Our country is at the top of the most 'vaccinated' countries in Europe (in July 2021 it would have been 90%, after which that percentage was sharply reduced, presumably to continue 'justifying' the ongoing lockdown and other measures). Since the injections have been declared untouchable and sacrosanct, we can expect the now so predictable nonsense statement from the mainstream media that it is all the fault of a Covid variant, and 'therefore' more 'vaccinations' are needed soon.

This kind of proven lies are still swallowed whole in the EU - partly thanks to all kinds of uncritical government 'useful idiots' from well-known TV programs - although slowly more people are starting to realize that in the past two years a lot of statements about corona / Covid and the 'vaccinations' have been made that turned out to be false, and promises have been made that were not kept or were broken time after time.

Not only in the Netherlands, but also in Canada, things are threatening to go completely wrong for vaccinated people in the near future: official government figures suggest that most are indeed developing Vax-AIDS now that their immune systems have been downgraded to an average of MIN 81%. (See also our February 2 article: (/ Canadian figures confirm pandemic of vaccinated people: Effectiveness of Covid injections found not to be the claimed 95%, but MIN 425%).

Warnings by Pierre Capel proved justified: immune system is destroyed

Independent scientists such as Dutch professor of experimental immunology Pierre Capel have been warning since the summer of 2020 that the mRNA injections pose a huge potential health hazard, because they allow your own body to produce the very most toxic part of the coronavirus, the Spike protein. Politicians and parliaments, however, refused to listen to critical voices; mass 'injections' were to be made, as this would be the 'only solution'.

Now his fears appear to have been justified. In most people the immune system does not seem to return to its normal and natural state after the Covid injections. Unvaccinated people now have a demonstrably much better working immune system (at least 5 times stronger), also against all kinds of corona / Covid variants. With the vaxxers the opposite is true; the shocking degradation to MIN 81% came about by the following calculation:

Percentage of unvaccinated 'cases' (in Canada) - Percentage of vaccinated 'cases' / highest unvaccinated percentage / vaccinated percentage = state of the immune system. In numbers: 418.4 - 2220.23 = 1801.83 / 2220.23 x 100 = - 81.55%. (Earlier the same official statistics showed a disconcerting vaccine effectiveness of MIN 425%).

Absurd: The strong can do almost nothing, the weak can do anything

The average Canadian vaxxer therefore has only 18.45% of his immune system left to fight against all kinds of viruses, cancers, et cetera. The question is if and when the remaining 18.45% will also have disappeared, there will be no resistance left and all these people will have contracted AIDS.

Despite this, it is precisely those with an intact immune system who are now being excluded from parts of society with QR codes and vax cards, and those with a destroyed immune system in various stages who are once again allowed to do anything, and 'infect' each other with anything and everything. Which normally would not be a problem, but now the completely innocent Omicron variant, and even every simple cold that would cause no more than a runny nose or cough in unvaccinated people, can literally become life-threatening.

All arguments for all measures now crushed

In any case, the Canadian figures have undeniably crushed all arguments for vax passes, QR codes, and certainly for mandatory vaccinations, and should be reason enough for any politician who still has somewhat the interests of their constituents at heart, and not just those of Big Pharma and their own position, to step in and immediately stop administering these experimental gene manipulation injections disguised as "vaccinations.

Let's hope a miracle happens, and the immune systems of millions of vaxxers spontaneously recover with the utmost urgency. If not, we may well be on the eve of an unimaginable health disaster that will completely overwhelm our medical care, and which may be seized upon by the authorities to introduce the very harshest a most inhumane dictatorship we have ever known in our history.

According to researchers, the now-discovered VB variant of HIV would have remained undetected in the EU for more than two decades. This would have been found suddenly based on the database of HIV patients, and a dozen existing cases with unusually high viral load.

Really? Amidst the ever-increasing evidence of an upcoming Vax-HIV outbreak, a new virulent variant is "accidentally" discovered in top-vax EU, which has supposedly been around since the 1990s? With corona (which top scientists already said in the first half of 2020 that it contains clear elements of HIV, which could only have been deployed in a lab*) it should of course have nothing at all to do, let alone with the Covid injections.

52

Daily deaths?

In just one database already 3.2 MILLION cases with supposedly 'rare' side effects recorded - Are politicians who continue to enforce these 'vaccines' actually life-threatening criminals just in view of these numbers?

Figures from the official WHO database in Uppsala, Sweden, confirm once again the carnage caused by Covid-19 gene manipulation injections. In recent weeks, 68 people are dying every day because of these "vaccines. In addition, 3.2 million cases of vaxxers with supposedly 'rare' side effects have already been registered. If it is then considered that it is totally unclear to what extent this WHO database contains the equally shocking figures from the European EMA (EudraVigilance) and the American VAERS, then it can be safely assumed that the real number of victims of this vaxxicide (vaccine genocide) is much higher.

What is striking about the WHO database is that it too consists of a huge number of categories into which vax victims are divided. One 'main' side effect such as 'impairment' is always broken down into many subdiagnoses that actually amount to the same thing. Why this is done is obvious; to keep the numbers visually as low as possible, which has an age-old misleading psychological effect. Consider Action, for example; most items are priced so low that customers quickly fill up their entire basket. After all, "it's all so cheap. At the checkout, they suddenly come out with a hefty amount.

Databases create false sense of security

If someone wanted to study all the diseases and conditions that fall under the categories mentioned, it would take months. So even if the authorities were to closely monitor the supposed 'safety' of the Covid gene manipulation 'vaccines', they would not be able to, given the gigantic amount of data and the way it has been compiled.

Thus, these databases seem to be designed primarily to give the public the false impression that everything is being monitored properly. In reality, no one is monitoring the security of the Covid-19 injections at all, because no one can.

Bear in mind that what side effects are reported come mainly from independent and/or conscientious medical personnel, and not from those who are paid, directly or indirectly, to sell these "vaccines" as "safe" and "effective" to the public. This is one of the main reasons that the European EMA/EudraVigilance contains only 6% of the actual number of victims, and the US VAERS database only 1%. Reporting side effects is severely discouraged and made almost impossible for physicians in many ways (such as extremely high administration per case).

Human suffering is deliberately covered up

In the WHO database, too, the search for concrete cases, i.e. concrete human suffering, is in vain. Almost everything is concealed beneath cold, medical or scientific terms that are meaningless to most people. This deliberately creates a distance between side effects and the victims, who are thus essentially dehumanized. As if they were nothing more than 'bad luck', nothing more than annoying 'numbers', and not persons who were ever healthy or ever lived.

Take, for example, two recent autopsies on two teenagers who died suddenly in their sleep from acute myocarditis, a recognized side effect of the Covid injections (in this case from Pfizer). Where can it be found in the database that the hearts of two core healthy young people were fatally damaged by these Pfizer gene manipulation injections? Nowhere.

Charts based on official figures unmistakable

That does not mean that there is no useful info to be gleaned from this data gang. Entrepreneur and analyst Erik Boomsma did it before with the European EudraVigilance, by digging it all out - a huge job. A ScienceFiles team did the same with the WHO database, mainly to see if there is indeed a statistical link between the increasing number of people who have been "vaccinated" and the ever-increasing number of reports of adverse reactions.

And indeed, even in these weeks the signs are unequivocal, and there are numerous blood diseases,

55

heart diseases, autoimmune disorders (such as Guillain-Barré syndrome) and serious illnesses attributed to 'Covid-19' that are the direct result of these 'vaccine' gene manipulation injections.

Such disproportionate increases are a strong, undeniable indication that there is a direct causal link to the ever-increasing number of people who have been injected in the past year. In the past week, 53,392 reports of people with one or more adverse reactions following a Covid-19 'vaccine' have been added, bringing the total number in the WHO database alone to 3,258,829. 19,222 of these recorded people have died. In the past few weeks, an average of 68 people have died each day from a Covid 'vaccine'.

Vaxxicide

If we apply the percentages of Eudravigilance (6%) and the VAERS (1%), established by independent university research, to the number of deaths in the WHO database, we arrive at an actual number of Covid vax deaths of 320,367 and 1,922,200 respectively.

We can therefore safely say that in just over 1 year several hundred thousand people have certainly been killed with these gene-manipulation injections. That is not to mention the many times greater number of people who have suffered serious, often permanent side effects and diseases.

But if you then call that a vaxxicide (vaccine genocide), then you are a "conspiracy thinker," a "wacko. I'm sorry, but unlike politics and mainstream media, I cannot see even one senseless human being killed under false pretenses as 'collateral damage'. Every person who, under great pressure from government, employer or society, has allowed himself to be tricked into taking an injection against a common respiratory virus, of which certainly the latest variant is barely noticeable, is an unnecessary drama that could and should have been prevented.

And yet another family destroyed

After all, it would just be your partner, your child, your friend or your family member. Take, for example, the Canadian Chantelle Watt, whose 34-year-old perfectly healthy husband suddenly dropped dead not long after his Covid injections in the presence of their two young children.

On social media, Chantelle - like 90% of the rest of the people who automatically believed the government's lies - had still been a strong supporter of lockdowns, vaccinations and other measures. Until her husband dropped dead, and after autopsy it was revealed that his heart had suddenly been completely destroyed in a short period of time. It didn't take long for her to realize that the anti-vaxxers had been right all along:

'I was a sheep. I admit that flat out. Brandon and I believed strongly in the vaccine and looked smugly at protesters, conspiracy theorists and all anti-vax messages. As of November 5, my eyes have been opened. I owe it to Brandon to share why I believe he is now dead. What killed him, and why his daughters now have no father.'

'His heart was massively damaged. There was so much scar tissue, it literally couldn't make a beat. I had no chance of resuscitating him. The official report stated that his entire heart was damaged - not just one ventricle or one area - from top to bottom. Completely attacked, for several months. The virus that killed him was probably the mRNA vaccine.'

How can you call a government, a parliament, a scientific institute, a media body and all others - such as the implementers who put these syringes in people - who deny or downplay these shocking figures and human tragedies, and on the contrary continue to demand with great coercion that everyone be injected with the same life-threatening substances, other than

criminals?

Mass murderers?

Or at least accomplices?

The fall of Trudeau?

'This is not just a fight against Trudeau. He takes his orders from the WEF, as does Australia, New Zealand and Europe. This is a fight for the freedom of the peoples'

Friend and foe alike have marveled in recent weeks at how incredibly quickly Canadian Prime Minister Justin Trudeau lost his nerve over the massive trucker protest. With absurd responses, such as labeling the truckers as "Nazis, anti-Semites and homophobes," and insisting that they were a "tiny minority" while the trucker convoy was breaking all records, he was making himself increasingly unbelievable and impossible to watch on a daily basis. Even in his own party, things are now beginning to rumble. The AI model of American economist Martin Armstrong predicted a "panic crisis" in politics in 2022 years ago, with Canada leading the way. Is the moment of Trudeau's fall indeed near, and if so: how many lackeys and errand boys of Klaus Schwab - we also think of our national WEF regime Rutte/Kaag - will follow?

As an internationally recognized top economist, Armstrong has personally shaken hands with Schwab and looked him in the eye, he writes. 'I doubt that many people who talk about him understand the true nature of his agenda.' Trudeau began following Schwab's orders in 2018, and the same can be said of many other Western leaders, such as Rutte and Kaag. In this context, Armstrong points to a WEF video in which

Australian Prime Minister Morrison promises to destroy the economy with rock-hard lockdowns so that Schwab can brutally push through his 'stakeholder economy', 'climate change' and an end to all things 'fossil' (= prosperity and freedom).

'No one is elected to carry out the Great Reset'

'These elected people do NOT represent the people,' Armstrong continued. 'NO ONE campaigned with this (Great Reset / Build Back Better) agenda. To get elected they lie, and then they take orders from the World Economic Forum. All the countries that have oppressed their people the hardest with this (Covid lockdowns, social distancing restrictions, enforced vaccinations, etc.) are being controlled by Schwab!'

Schwab tries with all his might to impose his (Marxist) economic theories on the world, and does so in a much more direct way than Karl Marx. Like the communists, the WEF top man wants to gain total control over all companies, and start deciding what they can/should produce, how much, under what conditions, and whether they should continue to exist at all.

Pension funds sucked dry for senseless climate projects

An important part of this is the complete draining of pension funds. Those of the Netherlands were by far the richest in Europe, but have been expertly handed over by the Rutte regime - and largely unseen by the media and the people - to the EU and the WEF in order to prop up the euro and to finance the equally costly and devastating climate agenda, which must lead to a rock-hard communist European Superstate dictatorship.

Australian pensions are now suffering the same fate. The largest pension fund, according to the Financial Times, will 'invest' €27.3 billion in Britain and the EU, according to Armstrong purely 'in loss-making projects (= climate/green energy projects), in order to help the collapsing Europe and ignore their own people. Of course they put a different spin on it, but there is no reason to invest in Europe now that it is in serious (financial-economic) trouble.'

'Schwab's grip on countries must be broken'

Canadian truckers have excellent timing, the economist continues. 'They need to break the grip Schwab has around the throat of Canada (and the Netherlands).' Meanwhile, the trucking protest has expanded further. For example, towing companies are refusing to work for the government and tow truckers away. 'They need to bring the government to its knees. Even his own party is starting to crack down. Trudeau is weak and a fool by listening to Schwab, who doesn't care about his future at all. All that matters to Schwab is imposing his economic theories on the whole world.'

'This is NOT just a fight against Trudeau. He takes his orders from the WEF, as does Australia, New Zealand

and Europe. This is a fight for the freedom of the peoples.'

'Those who support people like Biden and Trudeau (and Rutte, Kaag and Timmermans) have no clue. They are sheep who refuse to open their eyes to the fact that this is a serious international conspiracy to enforce the economic philosophy of a terribly sick man by undemocratic means. This is not a conspiracy theory. This is the best organized conspiracy to take over the world, going far beyond anything ever seen in James Bond movies.'

The same strategy was used at the time to introduce the euro, the currency that would have been rejected by every European people if it had been put to a referendum.

The German chancellor Helmut Kohl admitted ruefully afterwards that he would have lost such a referendum with 70% of people voting against it, and therefore introduced the euro for purely ideological reasons (the next step towards a European Superstate).

But "the collapse of the euro is probably inevitable around 2026/2027," Armstrong warns. 'With exactly the same strategy, these world leaders are now trying to push through Schwab's 2030 (Great Reset) agenda, without EVER allowing the people to vote on it, or even realizing that this agenda exists.

They call it a conspiracy theory, so that the people will remain blind to the same concept and strategy that created the euro.'

'Journalists who support him are Marxists and traitors'

Any journalist who denies this agenda is, in his view, a Marxist in disguise. 'They have no respect for our future, our human rights, or anything that makes it worth living. We were born with inalienable rights (like the right to self-determination over our own bodies and our own health, which is now being trampled on), not to be economic slaves under a central power.' Journalists who are behind the WEF agenda, then, he calls "traitors.

'This is a conspiracy to make us slaves to the deranged economic theories of a man who has indoctrinated the world in extraordinarily clever ways,' Armstrong concludes. 'And I've looked into his eyes face-to-face. Most commentators can't say that.'

Bankrun in Canada?

Next phase coup World Economic Forum against the West launched in Canada

Canada's left-liberal Prime Minister Justin Trudeau has finally revealed himself to be a rock-hard fascist dictator by declaring martial law against the perfectly peaceful and widely supported trucker protests. His extreme decision that the government may now seize people's bank accounts at any time without a court order seems to have caused an immediate bank run in the country, according to some as yet unconfirmed reports.

According to numerous social media posts, so much money is being taken out of banks that the websites of all of Canada's major banks (Royal Bank, Bank of Montreal and CIBC Bank) are all offline right now.

'On my way home, I stopped at the bank to take out all my money except enough to have direct debits like insurance,' someone Twittered. 'I heard the couple in front of me, Eastern European, also requesting hundreds of thousands. Only two customers, almost half a million. Good job, junior!'

Now that the Canadian regime has become a totally lawless tyranny and has effectively outlawed the people, citizens no longer trust their governments and banks. Rightly so, many think that if the government can just confiscate the money collected for the truckers and block their accounts, the same can happen to them if they dare to disagree with Trudeau.

Canadians, by the way, are also no longer allowed to leave the country freely. This is also only allowed if all of Trudeau's strict rules are met. Social media is now strictly censored just like in China. Freedom of expression has completely disappeared - except, of course, for those who proclaim Trudeau's "opinion.

Soon the EU and the US too if the WEF gets its way

What is going on in Canada, namely the next step in the coup by Klaus Schwab's human-hostile World Economic Forum, can also be expected in the short to medium term in the United States and the European Union. After all, the WEF's slogan reads:

'You'll own nothing'.

And that 'nothing' includes, in addition to your finances and possessions, ALL your freedoms and control, including the right to decide over your own body and health.

You can forget the 'you'll be happy' part. The only ones who will be happy about this are the current powers-that-be, with Klaus Schwab, Bill Gates and George Soros at the forefront, plus all their lackeys in national and international politics.

Canada has now been "chosen" to usher in a new phase towards the very harshest, most inhumane communist dictatorship this planet has ever known. I can tell you that this could also happen in the Netherlands if citizens, companies, institutions and law enforcement do not peacefully rise up en masse and say NO to this deliberate destruction of everything built up after the Second World War.

Besides, who believes - except the usefull idiots and all the profiteers of these sick states - the daily empty promises of 'our' leaders? I have heard so many people who have become rabidly ill after the booster shot, for whom this is really the last straw for their last bit of faith. 'It didn't help at all! They just lied. With me, the syringe won't come back in!' Or 'I've had four tests in a row; two were positive, two negative. They can just watch it with their quarantine, this really doesn't make sense anymore.'

In Europe, war with Russia seems to become the pretext for pushing through the Great Reset once and for all - Postponement?

As we have written many times, the bankrupt Western governments are desperately seeking pretexts such as the Covid plandemic to impose the communist "Great Reset" dictatorship on their countries. We have also regularly warned that large-scale protests - whether spontaneous or orchestrated - can be used as a pretext to declare a state of siege in order to push through the WEF Reset once and for all.

Indeed, that now appears to be what is about to happen with the Freedom Convoy in Canada, which we have been cautiously reporting on from the beginning. Prime Minister Justin Trudeau is in fact considering declaring Martial Law. In Europe, a false-flag war with Russia would be the perfect opportunity for our governments to crush our last shreds of freedom. In other words, the sledgehammer blow we have warned about many times seems to be coming.

The Canadian tyrant is said to have convened his cabinet last night for the possible activation of the Emergencies Act, making the state of emergency / state of siege a reality.

Today he would talk to all the prime ministers about this. If they agree, then Trudeau could use extreme force to end the Freedom Convoy, which has been completely peaceful, which damaged nothing and which enjoys overwhelming popular support.

'Temporary' emergency laws never go away by themselves

Since 2020, we have been able to see what happens to so-called 'temporary' emergency laws: they never go away. Should Trudeau indeed plunge his country into Martial Law, then the Canadian people have only one thing left to do to regain their freedom: try to depose him with all possible means.

Unfortunately, even such a popular uprising cum revolution seems to play right into his hands - unless the resistance is so massive and united that the police and army also side with the citizens.

Paris: Tear gas against peaceful protesters

In France, as part of the European variant of the Freedom Convoy - so far a pale shadow of the Canadian original - mass demonstrations were dealt with with tear gas in Paris, with innocent families sitting on terraces also becoming the victims. Trudeau's fellow dictator Emanuel Macron will most likely be rubbing his hands together, as this will give him another weapon to declare statehood in France as well.

City of 'Lady Liberty' rapidly turns into totalitarian World Economic Forum hellhole

Every day 1300 people abandon left-liberal New York and leave for right-wing Florida, where there are hardly any Covid measures and freedom still exists. New York is one of the textbook examples of the totalitarian 'Great Reset' dictatorship that Klaus Schwab's World Economic Forum is trying to impose on the whole world, but especially on the West.

Governor Kathy Hochul proposed new 'regulations' around Christmas that can be called nothing short of tyrannical, and which the state's Public Health Council will vote on soon. If it agrees, the stakes are high, as people may be arbitrarily arrested on the street, and children in school may be forcibly vaccinated without their parents' consent.

Mayor Eric Adams has already fired more than 1,400 civil servants, police officers, firefighters and over 900 teachers for refusing to be injected. Meanwhile, everywhere you go in New York, you are immediately treated aggressively by self-proclaimed BOAs and other law-abiding "Vaxxistasi" employees as soon as you dare to leave your mouthguard down for a few seconds too long after taking a sip of your drink.

Armed robberies are taking place in broad daylight in previously safe neighborhoods and streets. In Soho, an expensive boutique was stormed and robbed for about $50,000.

Forced vaccinations children in schools

And that's just the beginning of the misery, as Governor Kathy Hochul's newly drafted Covid regulations are about to be implemented. Without parliamentarians being able to vote on it, the Public Health Council is now considering an extreme law that will allow the state to arbitrarily label ANYONE a "health hazard" and arrest them. Moreover, arrestees have no rights whatsoever thereafter. 'Dissidents' - including freedom protesters - can then be arrested and imprisoned without trial.

In addition, the governor may make the permanent wearing of mouth masks mandatory, and ban all visits to nursing homes.

In addition, schools will be allowed to forcibly "vaccinate" students without parental consent, and thus inject them with the life-threatening Covid-19 gene-manipulation injections that have proven to be a threat. In addition, the New York State Board of Regents is going to vote on a blanket vaccination requirement for everyone.

'Schwab uses health everywhere as a means to impose Marxism'

'New York is descending into total pandemonium,' concludes American economist Martin Armstrong (1).

70

'This is part of Schwab's agenda - using health as a means of imposing Marxism.' Here again is the authentic image of Schwab in his office, where he has a statue of Lenin.

And from this man the Dutch VVD66 regime is now implementing its complete 'Great Reset' / 'Build Back Better' agenda, which is also turning our country step by step into a totalitarian climate-vaccination dictatorship in which 'you'll own nothing' (but the government/banks/pharma complex everything, even YOUR body and YOUR health).

WEF can be labeled a terror organization

Armstrong therefore calls the WEF a "foreign entity whose overt objective is total control of the world and the overthrow of the United States" (as well as the European democracies, insofar as they are still worthy of that designation at all).

Contributing to and implementing the WEF-Great Reset agenda therefore amounts to treason of the people and the nation, the perpetrators of which in politics, institutions, science and health care should be tried by a military tribunal.

It is therefore quite conceivable that the WEF should be officially labeled an international terrorist organization that is many times more dangerous than ISIS, Al Qaeda, Hezbollah and all other extremist Islamic groups combined.

71

Photon detector developed

Radarchip may later be built into smartphones - New tech contributes to smart grid that turns our entire planet into a giant digital prison from which escape is impossible.

While in some countries the Covid measures are being eased - most likely only temporarily - or even lifted, the work of building a transhuman totalitarian (bio)tech-controlled society continues unabated. Scientists at the University of Sydney are developing a photon radar, which can be used to scan objects and also human bodies at great distances.

The device, which works not with radio waves but with light waves, is so sensitive with its ultra-high resolution (1.3 centimeters) that it can detect location, speed and position (angle) with centimeters accuracy. In combination with the 5G nanotech injected via 'vaccines', it can be used to set up a watertight control system from which nothing or no one will ever be able to escape.

The 'advanced photonic radar' can, for example, continuously monitor whether someone is breathing and how high someone's heart rate is. The technology can therefore also be used in hospitals.

One radar can thus monitor all patients simultaneously (as well as everyone else in the hospital). The physical link to one's own external monitor will therefore no longer be necessary for all patients.

Radar based on light waves

Traditional radar systems work with radio waves of different frequencies. The higher the frequency, the more detailed an object - for example, an aircraft - can be imaged. However, high-bandwidth radars are complex and very expensive.

The Australian team has come up with a solution for this: a radar based on light waves. 'We actually use a photonic trick to generate such a high-bandwidth radar, without the need for very fast electronics,' explained Professor Benjamin Eggleton, principal investigator and director of the Nano Institute at the University of Sydney. 'And that's the magic.'

The photon radar, which has an extremely high resolution of 1.3 centimeters, is said to be harmless to humans and animals, and is first being tested on toads. If the tech is deemed safe, tests on humans will follow. Once an advanced prototype is developed, a mini version could be put into smartphones, the scientists claim.

Escape from the under construction smart grid impossible

Together with the 5G (later 6G) 'smart grid' that is being constructed worldwide and the nanotech injected into billions of people via 'vaccines', the entire world, including all objects and all people, will soon be monitored, controlled and even directed or 'corrected' in real time by A.I. systems. The entire planet will thus become one large permanent digital prison in which there will no longer be any form of privacy, and 'freedom' will be bound by very strict rules.

In metaphysical terms, you could even conclude that a kind of 'god' is being created: 'I see everything and at every moment, and know exactly what you are doing and thinking.'

Tech that allows thoughts to be read and controlled has been in development for years (see, among others, our December 23, 2021 article: Court sentences Harvard professor with patent on 5G mind control nanotech that can be injected with vaccines), as well as 'pre crime' systems that could predict if and where someone will commit a crime.

In any case, absolute obedience ('worship') of this A.I. 'god' will soon be very easy to enforce - except for those who have not allowed themselves to be injected/genetically manipulated, and refuse unreservedly to be included in this 'grid'. They will be branded as unwanted dissidents, and are already in danger of being removed from society (= this life) with the hardest possible methods within a few years.

Who will put an end to this globalist elite?

In any case, the Pentagon is already rubbing its hands with glee over the new photon radar, for surely you don't think that this wonderful technology will be used on a large scale for the benefit of mankind? That may only happen when this complete anti-human globalist Rockefeller-Rothschild power elite, with its infamous heads Bill Gates, Klaus Schwab and George Soros, along with their institutions such as the WEF, the UN/WHO, the IPCC, NATO and the IMF, have been removed from the scene.

But who is going to do that, now that virtually every government and administration - especially the Dutch - is completely in their power and dancing to their tune? Perhaps some hope can be drawn from the fact that this unrestrainedly greedy and thoroughly corrupt club of national and international administrators is now driven purely by deception, lies, deceit and betrayal, and for that reason there will be no real trust between them.

Therefore I think that sooner or later the globalists will turn against each other and attack each other like ferocious beasts. I only fear that this will be accompanied by terrible wars and unimaginable numbers of victims if the peoples do not manage to regain their freedom and self-determination in a very short time.

Space time terror?

Super particle accelerator allegedly used for weather manipulation and attempts to change timeline, according to some theories.

While everyone has been distracted by the war in Ukraine, the fear of a Third World War with Russia, and the impending financial crash that will set in motion the "Great Destruction" and then "Great Reset" to install a global totalitarian climate-vaccine dictatorship, something has been happening in the background that provides fodder for both old and new speculation about opening portals to other dimensions.

Indeed, the Large Hadron Collider at CERN (European Council for Nuclear Research) has been restarted. Located on the border of Switzerland and France, this largest superparticle accelerator in the world is more powerful than ever after a 3-year upgrade. According to some theories, the collider has been used for several years for attempts to manipulate the weather, and even to change the timeline.

Spectacular discoveries

The €7.5 billion LHC, by far the most expensive scientific instrument in the world, was built between 1998 and 2008, reaching an unimaginable energy of 13 TeV (teraelectron volts) in 2015. CERN scientists have been conducting unique particle experiments with it since 2009-2010 and have discovered several startling things over the years, including the famous Higgs boson ("God particle") in 2012.

Physicists at the LHCb experiment discovered last year that reality is probably structured differently than we think. The findings of the High Energy Physics experiment (hep-ex) 'Test of Lepton universality in beauty-quark decays' more or less boil down to the fact that nature seems to have an unknown (fifth) fundamental force, which would undermine the standard model used so far.

In January, the LHCb is said to have detected so-called X particles from the very first few seconds of the birth of the universe. This has been called "one of the greatest recent scientific discoveries.

In 2025, the High-Luminosity LHC (HL-LHC) project will begin, designed to make the accelerator even more efficient to collect more data from the experiments. Incidentally, in 2019 CERN came up with the plan for an even much larger particle accelerator, the 100-kilometer Future Circular Collider, which should cost around 10 billion. In comparison, the LHC is "only" 27 kilometers long.

Weather manipulation experiments

Because CERN has previously conducted experiments creating artificial clouds to better understand climate change, some claim that the "machine" is secretly being used to manipulate the weather.

'Doomsday machine'?

Science fiction-like speculations that the huge circular particle accelerator could be used to open destructive black holes or, on the contrary, portals to other dimensions, are usually laughed off by scientists.

Nevertheless, at the time a group of scientists tried to prevent the commissioning of the LHC 'doomsday machine' because the experiments could produce so-called 'black holes', which in the worst case could completely 'swallow up' the earth in 4 years. The attempt failed, but nevertheless the collider soon had to be shut down due to technical problems.

CERN scientist suggests gateway to other dimension

After the false start in 2008, the Large Hadron Collider was brought online in 2009. When an unexplained spiral-like phenomenon was filmed in the night sky in Norway in December of that year, some people linked it to the start-up of the particle accelerator at Geneva.

All sorts of wild theories surfaced about it; for example, the device was actually said to be a giant "Stargate," a gateway to another dimension from which aliens or other entities could possibly emerge.

Initially, such stories were hardly taken seriously by anyone, until CERN scientist Sergio Bertolucci astonished friend and foe in 2010 with his statement

that the collider could indeed open a door to another dimension "from which something could emerge," according to his literal description.
Later he is said - possibly under pressure - to have downplayed his statement by stating that by "something" he meant only unknown new particles.

At the end of 2010 the accelerator was in the news again when internal CERN documents revealed that the risk of dangerous subatomic particles being released during the experiments was much higher than officially admitted.

Nobel laureate Dr. Frank Wilczek even warned that the collider could produce so-called negative strangelets that would cause our entire planet to contract into an ultra-dense ball only 15 kilometers thick. CERN noted that it built a special device, the CASTOR, to detect these strangelets.

Return Annunaki, the devil, or the antichrist?

In front of CERN's main building - which has "666(/6)" in its logo - is a statue of the Hindu deity Shiva, the god of time, destruction and transformation. This religious image is said by some to symbolize CERN's secret efforts to open other dimensions, and specifically to open a "portal" for the return of the Annunaki (an alien race, according to esoterics) to Earth.

Others thought (/think) that the 'machine' will actually open a 'gateway' to the 'underworld', the dimensional abodes of dark beings called 'demons' and 'devils' in the Bible.

In Christian circles at the time, the story went around that the devil / Lucifer, 'the antichrist' and/or his 'spirit' would emerge from the portal, after which he would take over power over the entire world. Since that does not seem to have happened yet, these old speculations will probably be revived with the restart of the LHC.

Other world/time lines

Another "fantastic" theory is that a form of time travel would have been discovered with the LHC. Early this century, one John Titor appeared on alternative channels claiming to be a time traveler from 2036. He said that the LHC would lead to the discovery of other "world lines" (timelines), and therefore a form of time travel. He also predicted things like nuclear war, which (so far) have not come to pass.

In 2009, Titor was allegedly exposed as a hoax, but nevertheless, the military insignia he allegedly brought from the future is reminiscent of the loading screen of the CERN website in 2019, which had quite a few similarities to it.

Deceiver or not, mathematical physicists such as Irini Aref'eva and Igo Volovich suggested that at some point the LHC will become powerful enough to bend ("warp") space-time and create wormholes. This would make it possible to travel back in time to the moment the machine was turned on.

With this warp tech, it would also theoretically be possible to manipulate and alter the existing space timeline to lead it to a certain 'desired' outcome. There are speculations that this is already being done in order to pre-empt a great 'awakening' of the world, and from a religious perspective, to prevent an expected and foretold intervention of God, or the Light. This 'end time' in this case would then not end with a promised redemption, but would plunge humanity - at least, the part that will survive this apocalypse - into a horrible 'eternal' prison.

Hong Kong killing

Hong Kong, with a "zero Covid" policy, has adopted strict lockdown measures, such as closing schools and playgrounds. A new decision to traumatize children and teach them to be completely obedient to the authorities is the mass slaughter of hamsters, a few of which supposedly tested positive for Covid-19 in a pet store.

Since it has long been known that those tests give completely fake results worldwide, the question arises whether this hamster genocide is not a prelude to a planned genocide of all unvaccinated people.

The government wants to kill all hamsters born between December 22, 2021, and January 7, 2022, because the hamsters might be "contagious" to humans. Medical official Edwin Tsui, incidentally, acknowledged that this rarely happens, and it is more likely that the two employees of a 23-year-old pet store were infected by other people.

The AFCD (Agriculture, Fisheries and Conservation Department) now wants hamster owners to have their pets euthanized. Anyone who turns in their hamster must sign a statement that this is being done on a voluntary basis.

Hong Kong residents are used to regular protests against totalitarian measures, and have already formed numerous protest groups online. Hundreds of people have offered to take care of pet store hamsters.

Hamsters now, unvaccinated soon?

Michael Tien, a member of the Legislative Council, even thinks all hamsters should be confiscated and put down. 'Is this a drill for when they start cracking down on unvaccinated people?" wonders American economist Martin Armstrong. 'There is no medical reason to introduce such cruel laws.'

I think he is right. This is another test to see how people will react to killing living beings because of a supposed 'virus'. In this respect we have been conditioned in the EU for some time with the mass slaughter of (poultry) cattle on farms, euphemistically called 'culls'. For example, mink supposedly infected with 'Covid-19' were culled en masse in 2020. Earlier this month, 189,000 chickens were killed on two poultry farms in Bentlo because of the alleged presence of bird flu.

The slaughter of domestic animals, as in Hong Kong, is the next step towards genocide of all unwanted 'creatures' who refuse to follow the government-imposed false totalitarian Covid/lockdown/vax narrative.

Or in other words: the unvaccinated (still 1 in 6 on average in the west).

In the EU, too, there have already been suggestions on social media that 'infected' pets should be compulsorily culled. According to the government, the chance of 'infection' by your pet is very small.

Does ALL life have to disappear sometimes?

That animals can get a respiratory virus is nothing new, and is in itself THE proof that 'zero Covid', or even just 'containing' corona, is complete nonsense because such a virus can never be eradicated - unless you intend to make (almost) ALL life on this planet impossible.

Given the West's insane, counterproductive climate and energy degradation policies, and certainly the equally mendacious, devastating lockdown-social distancing-'vaccination' coercive measures, plus the longstanding unrelenting, and currently ramped up to extreme levels, drive to provoke a major war with one of the world's two largest nuclear powers, I'm starting to get the feeling that this may indeed be the underlying goal.

Whether the members of the WEF/WHO regime Rutte and of its yes-man fake parliament are aware of this, and/or perhaps even collaborate in it, they can best answer for themselves.

Russia protects Iranian arms shipments to Syria, leaves Israel powerless - Kremlin draws defensive line around Syria; Joint patrols Russian and Syrian air forces.

A potential game changer has quietly taken place in the Middle East. Russia has in fact begun actively protecting Iranian arms shipments to Syria from long-standing Israeli bomb and missile attacks. The Russians also used electronic weapons to disrupt Israeli GPS systems for some time yesterday, affecting civilian flights to Ben Gurion Airport near Tel Aviv. As Russia begins to more actively protect ally Syria, the Jewish state is rendered virtually powerless. Indeed, Jerusalem will never risk war with Russia, even with the almost automatic support of the U.S. at its back.

Israeli intelligence analysts call letting Iranian arms shipments land at the permanent Russian air base at Hmeymim near Latakia a "major concession to Iran, and the third setback for Israel in a week.

The Kremlin has long turned a blind eye to Israeli airstrikes on Syrian targets because the Iranian ammunition and arms shipments to the Islamic terror group Hezbollah in Lebanon were the target, rather than the Syrian army. However, that has already suffered so much damage from the shelling of Israeli warplanes that the Russians - after warning Jerusalem several times - now seem to have decided that enough is enough.

Joint air force patrols; defensive line around Syria

Syrian President Assad hopes that the Russian army will now also deploy its advanced S-300 and S-400 anti-aircraft missiles against the Israeli air force. Moscow does not seem to want to go that far yet, but that decision is now much closer. These missiles can destroy Israeli fighter planes in their own airspace.

On January 24, Russia and Syria already announced joint air force patrols over the Euphrates (border with Iraq) and the Golan Heights (disputed border with Israel). Two days later, the Russian army posted armed military police at the port area of Latakia.

These units would actually consist of special forces, which appear to be deployed because of the Israeli missile attacks on December 7 and 27 on the container port of Latakia. Iranian weapons destined for Hezbollah were allegedly stored there.

Warning to US

The Kremlin has now clearly raised a defensive line around Syria, of which, incidentally, Israel has not been officially informed. The stepped-up Russian protection may also be related to the Ukraine crisis, and could be taken as an additional warning to Washington that any war provoked by the US/EU/NATO will not be limited to just that country.

Syria is one of President Putin's greatest recent foreign successes. By intervening quickly and forcefully, he was able to prevent an almost certain Third World War started by Bush after supporting ISIS during the Iraq war, and in the years that followed, to precipitate the CIA-created and directed ISIS terror war to topple Assad. Many military analysts therefore agree that IS(IS) was defeated not thanks to the Obama administration.

Great reset = great fail?

The 'Build Back Better' of the 'lunatic from Davos' will totally fail after 2022 - Protesting alone will not stop an authoritarian communist dictatorship in Europe

The communist coup against the West, as we have called the World Economic Forum's Great Reset ("Build Back Better") since 2020, was doomed to failure after this year anyway, but is already beginning to fail. Indeed, after the US Fed, the BoE (Bank of England) also raised interest rates. The European Central Bank cannot possibly follow suit after almost 8 years of zero/negative interest rates, as that would immediately cause the already shaky European economy to collapse. The alternative, however, yields exactly the same result in a different way, and will extremely impoverish the Europeans, and certainly the Dutch, partly thanks to the devastating Covid and climate measures, in a very short time. So enjoy the (false) prosperity we still have for a while, because these are literally the last days.

The BoE raised the interest rate to 0.5% because of the rapidly growing inflation directly resulting from the Covid plandemie measures. Since the ECB has already wiped out the European government bond market (as well as purchasing power, pensions, savings and most foreign investment) with negative interest rates since 2014, it cannot possibly follow suit without triggering an immediate chain reaction to an unprecedented crash. The skyrocketing inflation of the moment is just the very beginning of that.

The 'lunatic from Davos' and his 'Build Back Better' after WW-3

WEF top man Klaus Schwab has 'a death grip on Europe's throat' according to top American economist Martin Armstrong. Through his 'Young Leaders' program and other forums (with Sigrid Kaag on the 'payroll', among others, and Prime Minister Rutte as a convinced supporter) he has - as he proudly told us a few years ago - infiltrated numerous governments around the world with his followers. Three WEF board members now sit in top positions at the head of the EU, the head of the ECB and the head of the IMF.

The Federal Reserve and Bank of England are now defending themselves against the WEF's frontal assault on Western economies and societies. 'This leaves the ECB alone with negative interest rates, defending Schwab's darkest visions for our future: the end of democratic governments and causing World War III so he can implement 'Build Back Better.'

Armstrong characterizes Schab as 'the lunatic from Davos who is changing the world', and is yet another academic who is going down the ever-failing communist path of Karl Marx; the path that promises the peoples a utopian state with permanent prosperity and security, but which always and everywhere leaves the citizens with the exact opposite, poverty and oppression.

'Schwab clings to the Marxist belief that academics are capable of redesigning the world economy. Like Marx, he believes he has the mental capacity to understand and reform the world. He has convinced world leaders (such as Mark Rutte) to listen to his nonsense, when it has been proven that everywhere it is tried, it goes wrong.'

Man himself will be changed forever

'But Schwab has convinced them that it will work this time, and they will gain even more power. Do any of these people, who are incompetent to rule the world, know anything about how economics works? Communism and socialism have always failed because we are human, and we are not worker bees that can be controlled from a central hive.'

That problem is well known to the current elite. Their solution: under the false guise of fighting a supposedly dangerous respiratory virus, inject people with gene-manipulating substances that will

1) incrementally wreak havoc on their immune systems, making them totally dependent on government booster shots, and therefore will not dare to resist, and where

2) contains graphene oxide nanoparticles that can assemble themselves into the basis of some sort of "operating system," which can remotely turn people into will-less slaves via 5G and AI. (As you know from our previous articles, this is definitely not an sf

conspiracy theory, but already developed tech that has been shown to be put into a significant percentage of Covid-19 injections).

EVERYTHING will be taken from citizens and businesses

'Big Tech is aligned with the dark forces to change this world and eliminate all our freedoms,' Armstrong continued. 'They are cancelling our freedom of speech to suppress any sound that dares challenge their ideas. Indeed, they have been promised that they will rise to the top, as long as they help destroy the very country where freedom allowed them to rise to the top.'

'Has their thinking been corrupted by money, or have they merely been lured into Schwab's dream that in the changed world they will be the new elite?'

Governments - despite the rapidly growing resistance, however impressive it may be at times, such as the Truckers protest in Canada - will never give up their power over society gained through disinformation and deception campaigns of their own accord. Meanwhile, especially in Europe, governments spend money like water, because they know that the 'Great Reset' default is coming, and in the new digital financial system ALL will be taken away from all citizens and SMEs (Schwab's 'You will own nothing...'). And by 'everything' they also mean control over your own body, health and even your own will and thoughts.

According to Armstrong, however, the Covid planemic
to reset the world economy will fail totally after 2022,
with horrific consequences. The current Western rulers
will then attempt to maintain and strengthen their grip
on society and the economy with unprecedentedly
harsh dictatorial coercive measures. This threatens to
plunge untold numbers of people into deep poverty and
misery, and to make unimaginable numbers of victims
(we must think of a planned population reduction of
25% to possibly 50%). The total collapse will then
probably follow in late 2024 - late 2025.

**An infamous trio that wants to plunge the whole world
into chaos**

'These three men think they know better than everyone
else,' the top economist argues.

The infamous 21st century 'antichrist' trio.

Armstrong: "They are destroying Western Civilization. In
the process, they deliberately cause the decline and
decay, thinking they can rebuild it in better ways. Sadly,
in doing so, they ensure that China and Russia will
become the stronger economies thanks to these bigots.'

'They think the world will survive only because of them,
as they see it. Our computer (Socrates A.I.) has
predicted the demise of their arrogant grandiose
visions. They will be remembered for generations, just
like Adolf Hitler.'

As I once wrote about our own politicians in 2020: If we survive this Great Reset coup as a people, the names Bill Gates, George Soros and Klaus Schwab will be cursed for generations, and for the next century no one will give their newborn children any of these first names.

Protesting alone will not help

Therefore, protests alone, such as the European Freedom Convoy in Brussels on February 7 and 14, no matter how good and necessary, will not help. What's more: they will be used by the elite to push through their objectives even harder and faster.

UNLESS the 'waking up' that has just begun is followed with the greatest urgency by an active NO, that is a massive (citizens, companies, and preferably also police and other officials) peaceful resistance in the form of a complete refusal to cooperate with ALL coercive measures (such as QR codes and 'vaccinations'), ignoring ALL devastating Covid- and climate dictates, and of its own accord restoring a free economy and society.

As yet, we see far too few signs of that much-needed awakening. But what is not, may yet come. Every day that those in power have to postpone their series of sledgehammer blows with which they want to bring us down completely, is an opportunity to at least delay, and perhaps even stop, the terrible future they have in store for us.

WEF: a danger to society?

WEF wants not only mandatory vaccinations but now also mandatory antibiotics (society is being deliberately addicted and therefore made totally controllable).

In one of his recent commentaries, the American top economist Martin Armstrong comes to the same conclusion that we drew in 2020: Klaus Schwab's World Economic Forum, with all of its "Young Global Leaders" and other loyal followers in the political elite of the West, is a threat to all of human civilization. Klaus Schwab himself boasted that he has now infiltrated all major governments, now controlling Europe, Canada, Australia and New Zealand. Not one nation has been given a vote on handing over virtually all power to this authoritarian Marxist, who has also gotten our government to partially dismantle our economy and incrementally end all our freedoms.

'We face a clear and present danger coming from various heads of state who are busy promoting the cancel culture, in order to suppress any opposition and change the future of us and our posterity,' Armstrong writes. 'Schwab, with his admiration for Lenin, with his Young Global Leaders - including Justin Trudeau - is imposing his communist ideas on the world, which means that democratic principles and the 20th century separation of power have been completely undermined, and replaced by Schwab's economic theories, of which he is openly very proud.'

'He does not allow people to vote on his dream, and indoctrinates state leaders to impose his agenda with purely authoritarian power... We see that the most authoritarian regimes that suppress the rights of the individual are all linked to Schwab, even Australia. This is a serious threat to the future of civilization. Schwab has managed to convince people to join his agenda, which he always portrays as (creating) fairness and equality, exactly like Marx and Lenin.'

The entire West plus the Vatican under Schwab's control

Even the White House he managed to take over; President Biden named his Build Back Better Act (HR 5376) after the infamous slogan of the WEF, which as far as we are concerned can be written more aptly as '6uild 6ack 6etter'.

Schwab and his 'club' think that historically failed communism everywhere and always will work if the whole world is controlled. In addition to the EU, including the Netherlands, the Vatican has also fallen for this fascist agenda; Pope Francis is a staunch communist, whose election was most likely brought about by manipulation (and presumably blackmail and outright coercion) from Freemasonry and the then Obama administration. Francis' main message, then, is invariably Schwab's "Great Reset" and the climate-vaccine agenda, which, in the eyes of the self-proclaimed "Holy See," would apparently suddenly be at the heart of God's plan with humanity.

Well, I agree with the Pope to the extent that it is indeed the plan of ONE 'god' with humanity. However, the name of this 'god' is Lucifer, also known as 'the Devil', Satan, 'the ancient serpent', the Dragon, the Demiurge, et cetera.

EU shadow president Soros wants to bring down China and Russia

One of his best known and most loyal lackeys is George Soros, given his enormous power and influence, the de facto shadow president of the EU, whose son is also a Young Global Leader at Schwab. Soros published a video in which he called 2022 a crucial year for supposedly "human rights," and therefore called for the overthrow of the Chinese government and President Xi Jinping, the Chinese president is probably the real antichrist so it will be interesting to see how the smoke and mirrors unfold.

Soros claims that he and his 'Open Society' are against authoritarianism, but just look at how he has managed to destabilize Europe and also the US with his left-wing hate and divisive agendas (packaged under 'diversity', 'Antifa', 'BLM' and 'defund the police', among others), which in some ways have made the West even more authoritarian than China (certainly Canada, Australia, New Zealand, Austria, Italy and by the looks of it also Germany).

Soros is exclusively vehemently opposed to anything conservative, right-wing and pro-freedom. In doing so, he, like most Western leaders and 'his' EU, uses the tactics of the infamous anarchist-satanist Saul Alinsky, by continuously accusing his enemies of exactly what he does himself, such as promoting authoritarianism, misleading and lying to the public with mis- and disinformation via the mainstream media, and extreme intolerance of other opinions and visions.

By the way, 2022 is indeed a political "Panic Year" in Armstrong's AI model. There are important elections in the US (mid-term), France and Australia, and Xi Jinping's term is coming to an end. The US mid-term elections 'are vital to stop Schwab's Agenda-2030 infiltration of the US....

A globalist sect

In 2020, we first spoke of a globalist climate-vaccine cult, which quite a few people found exaggerated. That it was nevertheless by no means hyperbole is now recognized by more and more analysts. Even Roger Koops (The Brownstone Institute) bluntly compares the WEF and WHO to a "sect that has penetrated the entire world.

Koops, who spent his entire professional career working in the pharmaceutical and vaccine industries and emphasizes that he is 'not a Covid denier,' writes that major manufacturers Pfizer, J&J, Moderna and Astra-

Zeneca were urging governments to buy their corona 'vaccines' as early as February. 'That was less than a month after the genetic sequence (or partial sequence) was made available by China... I thought the whole concept that a ready vaccine would be developed within a few months was ridiculous.'

He points out that infamous names like Bill Gates (/ the Gates Foundation), Neil Ferguson and Anthony Fauci were advocating lockdown strategies years ago. And since 2020, what do the implementers of those freedom-destroying policies - Joe Biden, Boris Johnson, Jacinda Ardern, Angela Merkel, Emmanuel Macron, Justin Trudeau, Xi Jinping, Mario Draghi, Scott Morrison, (Mark Rutte and Sigrid Kaag), have in common? 'They are all connected to the World Economic Forum... run by Klaus 'you will own nothing' Schwab and his family... the origin of the Great Reset and... Build Back Better.'

Society is being intentionally addicted to vaccines and antibiotics

Recently the WEF posted an article advocating the introduction of a 'subscription' to antibiotics, ostensibly to combat resistant bacteria. 'I think they have the same philosophy as with vaccines, which is absolutely the approach with the coronavirus: keep paying and taking the boosters... Get society 'hooked' on an intervention, effective or not, and then keep feeding them. This becomes especially effective if you can keep the fear in.'

Many times I have made the comparison to the science fiction series Star Trek - Deep Space Nine, in which a hostile alien race uses genetically modified warriors called the Jem'Hadar. They are controlled and kept absolutely obedient by being made addicted to a chemical substance called Ketracel-white, without which they suffer terrible physical and mental health problems and then die. The same concept is now being applied to the entire world's population with the Covid gene manipulation injections, and apparently a compulsory antibiotic addiction is being added.

What I also noted in 2020 is that from a business perspective this is the most brilliant revenue model ever. It guarantees Big Pharma trillions in revenue forever, and gives the governments that impose it on their populations unlimited permanent power and total control.

The survival of mankind is at stake

At the same time, this is probably the most diabolical conspiracy ever forged and executed against humanity, one that will forever change the complete future and nature of the human race - at least the small portion that will be allowed to survive the now-in-progress planned "end times.

After WW2, historians have long wondered what would have happened if Adolf Hitler had been stopped in time. The same question can - and should - now be urgently asked again about Klaus Schwab and his World

Economic Forum, because this time the survival of the entire human race may well be at stake. Are there any independent forces left on this planet with enough power and courage to eliminate the WEF for good? Or will we collectively allow ourselves to be plunged into this absolute worst hell on earth ever in the coming years almost without significant resistance?

Still exaggerated, do you think? In the context of 'from the mouth of the monster itself', please read our article from 2 days ago; New WEF report almost literally announces digital 'sign of the Beast' system.

Mark of the beast?

WEF wants to completely 'outsource' your decision-making power to an A.I. (= a digital 'god' is eventually going to control, direct and determine your entire life) - Social Credit system is inexorably coming: only access to services (such as bank account, health care and travel) if you exhibit the 'right behavior

In the brand new WEF report Advancing Towards Digital Agency, a digital 'sign of the Beast' system is almost literally announced. The WEF presents it as something wonderful: an 'intermediary digital agent' will soon take all your so-called difficult choices and decisions off your hands, so you no longer have to worry about them. In this scenario a data intermediary digital agent (your digital 'representative') takes on the role of decision-maker.

(Your) consent becomes automated... with the help of AI, the data intermediary agent autonomously decides what kind of data permissions someone would like to give. This opens the door to even more possible uses of that data' (p.12). The WEF readily admits that there are not only 'wonderful opportunities' here, but also 'significant risks.'

'This is moving towards a fully automated system of personal data collection and processing, to put "notice and consent" restrictions out of play (= all your personal info will be collected and shared outside of you with whomever.

So: END PRIVACY. Just read!:). This is a scary and fantastic area, and clearly not so different from a world where there are no data protection and privacy requirements at all: the difference is that there is a system, ideally with backstops (but so not necessarily = no brakes on it), designed in a human-centric way, and therefore preserves user preferences, and applies user restrictions accordingly.' (bold and underlined added)

Note the way the following is worded: 'In fact, there is no reason why AI agents could not be programmed to be conservative if that corresponds to the user's preferences.' The 'in fact' and 'could be' merely indicates the technological possibility, but clearly keeps open the possibility that another political choice could just as easily be made to NOT give you that say (anymore).

In fact, given what has been introduced and announced in the last few years in the area of data - think especially of the QR code and already decided upcoming digital EU identity - we can safely conclude that the chance that governments in cooperation with Big Tech, Big Pharma and Big Banks will decide for you and me how 'your' AI will be programmed and will deal with your data, is 100%.

A digital 'middleman' making decisions for you

On page 9 it says that your personal data will be stored in a 'vault' (digital safe). Your data intermediary (say, the digital 'intermediary' or 'copy' of yourself that makes the decisions for you) will then 'advise' you on the use of your data, 'including keeping track of who is using that data and for what purpose.' So you still just get the 'right' to see who all gets to see that data and why, but not to determine THAT it is or isn't. There is a very real chance that such a 'vault' will soon become mandatory, and that without this digital identity you will no longer be able to do anything at all.

One of the ways your personal data will be used is to "make a social impact, such as contributing to academic or scientific research. Well, in view of the gigantic fakescience fraud in the area of CO2 'climate change' and the Covid pandemic/injections, you can assume that those with the 'wrong' political beliefs, and/or refusers of the mandatory injections and 'climate' measures will very easily be branded in 'scientific' reports as a 'danger' to society, which will be used by politicians to contain or even remove those 'dangers'.

Your personal digital 'god

So the bottom line is that you are going to have some kind of personal digital 'god' who is going to make all the important decisions for you, because based on all your personal data, that 'god' would know exactly what you want and need, and when and where. And the 'reassuring' thing about this whole thing? Throughout the report, it is automatically assumed that the government is going to totally control ANY aspect of this process, this 'god', and therefore YOU.

Of course, these governments, always so 'reliable', will automatically share your information with other, according to them reliable' parties such as ministries, the EU, the WEF, the CIA, the AIVD and other intelligence services, to name but a few. After all, surely you want to stay 'safe'? Then we really need unlimited control over ALL your data. Surely you have nothing to hide from us? Because otherwise you might be seen as a 'threat'.

Just read what it says on page 16: 'A public body or government agency could take on the role of an intermediary, especially when it comes to data originating from public bodies.... However, whether a public body can be called 'reliable' in any given country will depend on the role of the government, and its degree of control, access and use of surveillance (monitoring) laws and related technologies.

'Legal Coercion'

As if this message were not enough - you get the idea: 'more control = more reliability and security' - it is also added that if there is no trust in the system, in the government and in its underlying intentions, no active use can be made of it, except under 'the force of law'. In this context there is also talk of a 'super-intermediary' that should make it possible to share data extensively between various cross-border participants. This will involve such an enormous amount of data that it can only be processed by a kind of super-AI.

We have had more than enough negative experiences with the 'force of law' at least since 2020 (lockdowns, mouth caps, social distancing, QR code), to which a European ID (/QR) will be added later this year, and the step-by-step expansion across the EU of compulsory 'vaccinations' under the duress of high penalties, as is now happening in Austria, the homeland of the infamous fascist with the moustache, whose dark mind is evidently making a big comeback.

On page 26, a case study focuses on the TDA (Trusted Digital Agent) 'Valexander', which is advertised as 'friendly and reliable'. This literally states that only the sharing of 'some sensitive or crucial data' will require direct human interaction, i.e. your consent. But who is going to determine what personal data gets that classification? From all indications, this will ultimately be the TDA itself, driven by the overarching AI, and of course input from governments.

In other words, the little bit of 'personal consent' you are left with has only been added for the sake of it, so effectively just like elections in the Netherlands are supposed to keep up the appearance of a 'parliamentary democracy'.

EVERYTHING will be linked to your digital ID

Your' digital ID will be linked to EVERYTHING: health care (including insurance), financial services (such as access to your bank accounts), food and sustainability, travel and mobility (= passport, buying tickets), humanitarian response ('to access services and show qualifications to work abroad'), E-commerce (to store and pay online), social platforms, E-government (including voting, which means that elections go digital and the outcome can no longer be trusted) and telecommunications.

Telecommunications include access to the Internet, use of your smartphone, and - note - to monitor (your) devices and sensors for their energy use, air quality, and traffic congestion. This means that your smartphone will be constantly connected to the overarching digital grid, which will, for example, see in real time if you are in a traffic jam, and thus know 24/7/365 where you are and where you are going. And if all goes well, you are aware that your smartphone does not have to be on to do this.

Embedded in your body

Smartphone? Surely there is a much better and more reliable way to make it depend on whether or not you have it in your pocket. Why not make it an implanted c.q. injected (nano) chip? That way your own body becomes your ID and payment card in one.

The WEF report also mentions this: Your digital profile 'may contain inherent data characteristics (such as biometrics)(= physical characteristics), or assigned characteristics (such as names or national ID numbers)'. Once this digital ID is in place and established, it will also include your purchasing and medical behavior, plus your 'assessments and decisions' based on your profile and behavior ('a bank decides an individual's attractiveness for a loan'). This is nothing less than the social credit system as rolled out in China.

Under the heading 'Future' (pg.23) it literally speaks of the 'next level of data intermediaries ('embedded in your body' = embedded in your body, devices, houses, cities, etc.)'. Of course, these include the 'vaccine passports' (pg.24, Box 4), which nobody wanted: 'These passports, by their very nature, serve as a form of digital identity.' It is acknowledged that personal health data is sensitive, but that 'vaccine data is an unimaginable asset for public health... In such cases, notice and consent (from the user) is not necessarily necessary to reuse the data...'

Schwab in 2016: 'This is absolutely going to happen within 10 years'

In a French TV interview in 2016, Schwab predicted that all this is 'absolutely going to happen in the next 10 years,' starting with (nano)chips in our devices and clothes, and then 'in our brains or in our skin. And eventually maybe direct communication between our brains and the digital world.

We see a kind of merging of the physical, digital and biological worlds.'

For regular readers, none of this is new. After all, we've been writing about this for years.

The possible use of (eventually mandatory) 'vaccinations' to build up the 'sign of the Beast' system IN your body, so that you will surrender your free will in ALL areas and will no longer be able to resist this A.I. 'god' in the making, we already predicted in 2009.

Creation System of the Beast completed in 2025?

Remember, in 2019 it was decided to accelerate this agenda, which was supposed to be realized by 2030, to 2025 ("The Accelerator"). This was most likely done because the global awakening that we are dealing with the darkest, most anti-human and downright diabolical agenda ever here is happening faster than what the WEF globalists had taken into account.

Presumably, other factors will have played a role, such as the obstruction of Russia and China, and Europe's rapidly eroding financial and economic position.

Conclusion: the WEF is making every effort to have the "system of the Beast" completed by 2025. Given the frightening geopolitical developments, it is certainly not inconceivable that 2025 will be brought even further forward (2023-2024) by means of a number of major wars - planned or unplanned (Ukraine-NATO/Russia, China/Taiwan, Israel/Iran, India/Pakistan), financial-economic crashes, major disruptions in the energy and food supply caused by 'climate policy'.

Re-education camps?

Chinese 're-education camps' as example: 'Muslims come out happier there' - Freedom of expression dies, even in the West

According to World Economic Forum Young Global Leader Wang Guan, a leading political journalist for a Chinese state propaganda channel in the U.S., opponents of Klaus Schwab's "Great Reset" will be put into "re-education camps" just until they give up "outdated" notions of freedom and nationalism (and, in some countries, the right to bear arms). And, we suspect, have unlimited numbers of injections put into their bodies, through which they will be gradually linked to a global transhuman A.I. network.

The WEF, as we know, seeks "the abolition of private property, a goal summed up in the controversial 'you will own nothing and be happy,'" as lead investigative reporter Natalie Winters (National Pulse) reiterates the pursuit of a totalitarian communist world government.

Truly everywhere, the wretched World Economic Forum has got its claws into. For example, the "weeping journalist" who almost demanded that Boris Johnson and NATO come to Ukraine's military aid, thus starting World War III against Russia, also appears to be a WEF Global Leader (2019) (as well as a Joe Biden campaign supporter). (5)

'Muslims happy out of re-education camps'

In a short video ("Punctuating Western double standards about Xinjiang"), Wang, one of 112 Young Global Leaders selected by Schwab, points to the "success" of Chinese re-education camps for Uyghur Muslims. Wang visited Xinjiang and talked to Uyghurs there, all of whom rejected international accusations that the Chinese government was committing genocide against them.

'54 countries, most with Muslim majorities, defended China's counter-extremist activities in Xinjiang. They praised China for its development policies there, and for 'taking care of its Muslim inhabitants,'" he explained. 'And they probably have a point.'

The video features several Muslims who had to spend months in such a reeducation camp. There they learned all kinds of new skills, which is why they are now working in various sectors. One of them is 26-year-old Rukiya Yakup, who was incarcerated for 10 months and during that time studied Mandarin and sales. Now she is a real estate agent earning more than 8,000 yuan a month (well above the local average). 'I feel happier now,' Yakup said. 'And I have a sizeable income.'

Freedom of speech is dying, even in the West

Freedom of speech, once so sacred in the West, is dying to make way for WHO/WEF ideology, the only 'opinion' you will soon be allowed to have. For example, in the US you may now be targeted as an 'extremist' if you believe that the election was stolen, or if you doubt the official Covid narrative. (3) The U.S. government allocates a whopping $2.6 billion for programs that spread 'disinformation' and 'hate'

And 'hate', these days, is just having any dissenting opinion, such as supporting Russia in its military operations against the Ukrainian neo-Nazi regime. Freedom of speech', but not to view Russian websites like RT, because they are blocked one by one by Western intelligence services.

Also in our own country there are plenty of examples, such as the condemnation and blocking of the magazine 'Gezond Verstand' of former Dutch newspaper journalist Karel van Wolferen. Recently the publisher Mediahuis Noord banned Forum voor Democratie advertisements from all newspapers and magazines. Dissenting opinions are in any case not done in the mainstream media, unless they are deliberately put in the spotlight with the sole purpose of undermining or even ridiculing them.